THE ENORMOUS DESPAIR

JUDITH MALINA

THE ENORMOUS DESPAIR

Random House New York

 Published in the United States by Random House, Inc., New York, and simultaneously in Canada by Random House of Canada Limited, Toronto.

Library of Congress Cataloging in Publication Data

Malina, Judith, 1926–
The enormous despair.

1. Living Theatre, New York. I. Title.
PN2297.L5M27 792'.097471 75-37063
ISBN 0-394-46961-5

Manufactured in the United States of America
98765432
FIRST EDITION

THE ENORMOUS DESPAIR

AUGUST 31, 1968:

Sailed at noon from Le Havre.
The *Aurelia,* an Italian ship.
A cruise ship chartered as a student ship to take American students home from European vacations.
The company reassembles from all over:
Jenny and Steve and Carl and Julian and I: who sailed together on the *Hanseatic,* which brought us to Europe:
And Isha leaving the continent of her birth to go to the continent of her citizenship.
Steve Ben Israel, Henry Howard and Nona, Jim Tiroff, Jim Anderson, Roy Harris, Mary Mary, Cal, Luke, Rufus, Diana, Gene and Michele, and Chiwe. And five Sharis plus Peter.
Going home. And also Mel Clay and Carol Berger, who are to join the company, and Peter and Karen Weiss, who hope to join.
And for the first time to America: Günter Pannewitz, and Odile and Tai, and Echnaton, and Gianfranco, and Pamela, Petra, Pierre Devis, Leo, Birgit, Rod, Sandy, Frank, and Margery.
And Ali and David and Ben.

Some are to come on board at Southampton.

Passengers include long-haired students, lots of square students, with that sad formal thing that square students have nowadays.
Paul Blackburn says he is "on the staff"; he complains he had to refund his tickets at Avignon, because we withdrew from the festival.

Farewells with Alain: he inscribes to Julian a copy of *La Révolte Etudiante*. Jenny sits on the floor, crying: "I read the

cards: We are in danger. We are in danger of falling under the power of a great king."
She is expressing everyone's paranoia. She says we're going to America to get killed.
Carl says: "When the boat stops, do you realize where we'll be?"
Rioting in Chicago.
Warfare in Nigeria.
Can't get the news on the radio.
Choppy Channel crossing. Gray weather.
All of us are uptight about the ship's rules.
The ship people are worried about people getting drunk.
They spoke to Carl about the dangers of "fornication." They feel responsible for the young people.
The captain says to Julian: "I like things square."
"I like things circular," Julian smiled.
"I have read a great deal about The Living Theatre," said the captain.

Steve comes in to describe what he read in the *International Herald Tribune* about Chicago.
How they beat up the students supporting McCarthy in the Hilton Hotel.
The Senator, awakened, amazed at the bloodshed, appealed to Mr. Humphrey, Vice President and presidential nominee, for help.
The Vice President's front man/press secretary/ said he wasn't interested.
Senator McGovern, another presidential aspirant, said that he never believed the stories about police brutality until now.

I try to write an essay on Piscator for *World Theatre* magazine, which is putting out a special Piscator issue.

Three nights I stayed up and forced myself to write, at least something. Reading it over tonight I find it worth tearing up. That tight style, and that rigid form in which Piscator expected us to write the "critiques" which he required for his weekly "Theatre Research" class.

SEPTEMBER 1, 1968:

Passing the gentle slopes of England/Penzance to Land's End/ the sky is blue with pleasant little gray clouds. The English radio can be heard by placing the antenna out of the porthole. It brings a terribly ethnic soap opera about ordinary English folks. Through the binoculars I see their houses. They are hearing this broadcast in those houses and imagining their landscape.
A rainbow appears over Land's End.
The radio, as it is Sunday morning, begins to pray.
The English Service.
I go downstairs to the theatre, where the ship's service is in progress. The preacher is a young theology student. He is reading from St. Paul:

> ". . . first the Jew, and the Greek, for God knows no partiality."

He apologizes for his sermon, then reads it nervously. It's not bad.
"We each have a bag," he reads, "and it's neither mixed enough, nor wide enough."
Reading from the mimeographed pages, we sing, to the tinkling piano, the traditional hymn of the sea.

Ship's "News Bulletin" brings news of threats/dangers to Romania by Russian troops.
It is written in USIA style.

There is a "Forum" in the big salon: they are discussing "Anti-Americanism: Is it dead and buried?"
The listeners and participants speak in a cool college-bred style—noncommittal and neutral. Surely they will decide that anti-Americanism is not dead, but that it is a problem that must be combatted.
In a nook behind this debating room a bunch with guitars are singing protest songs. They don't give a shit about the "Forum."

I listen to the bland remarks of the young Americans.
The strong voices of the *Enragés* ring in my ears. Their passion and their conviction, their strong feelings and their potency.
These American college students are so pale. They are so white.
Red and black anarchists glowing.

August 28, 1968:
On the Boulevard St. Michel and St. Germain des Prés, among the sidewalk artists ("I am a Finnish student. Please help me.") and sellers of jewelry and guitarists, there are two new sights:
—The *Enragés* selling books and radical literature, posters and pamphlets, Bakunin and Rosa Luxembourg.
They greet us. They know us from the

courtyard of the lycée in Avignon.
—A lanky barefoot young man sitting
on the sidewalk, leaning on the building
behind him. On the sidewalk a peace
symbol.
"I am a deserter from the American Army.
I am trying to make my way to Sweden.
Please help me." On the peace symbol, some
coins and two ten-franc bills.

That was a last flash of Paris: the protesting, burning faces and voices on the stage of the Odéon, the chanting youth marching with red and black flags down the Boul' Mich' when it belonged to them; the poetry of Avignon.

Then these pale white voices:

"Our cultural exchanges are gradually overcoming the old prejudices against the fat American tourist with his camera. Greater understanding between people is being established . . ."

Can't listen. Even Paul Blackburn says, "It's like wading through glue."

A few of us listen—Carl, Henry, Rod and I—but to speak is to be lost in the welter of containment that the atmosphere represents.

If I stood up and said anything they would say, "Thank you for the controversial remarks," and go on with their cool talk.

But last year everyone said the French students were a hundred years behind the English students, with their long hair (when no one in Paris had long hair except English tourists and some international beatniks), or the students at Berkeley.

And the Italian students were said to be irremediably

subservient to Church and Family, and they've
risen up.
And the German students and even the Swiss students, where they said it could never happen.

And any minute this bland debate could swell into Contestation.

The captain called Julian to his quarters and they drank Campari. He says:
"I have heard stories about you, that you are like wild animals who couple anywhere and any time, in the corners of the dining room or in the corridors."
Julian reassures him: "We talk of such things but we are really a very inhibited company."
Captain: "Not that I'm a puritan. I myself am a dirty old man, but there *are* all these young people on board."

I can't write the Piscator piece, just *because* I have something to say. And as far as Piscator goes I could never express myself to him, as I now can't express myself about him. My respect renders my style banal. I want only to praise him and am afraid to be critical. I tell myself that it is because I don't want to do him an injustice, but it may be that my schoolgirl fear of him, matched with my schoolgirl infatuation with him, makes me afraid. I don't want to displease him, or make daddy angry.*

The Battle of Algiers film: A primer of violence. Four hundred ways to kill police.
Brilliantly made, but too instructive. Too instructive? That isn't possible!

* ITI (International Theatre Institute), *World Theatre,* Vol. XVII, 4–5, "Piscator and the Documentary Theatre."
I never finished my essay.

Make the information available.
Traces the escalation from assassination to riot to war.
Isha sleeps in Julian's arms through this film about shooting and bombing.

The sea is rough. Many are seasick. At the *Ospedale* the nurse dispenses Valontan against seasickness. Jenny goes to the *Ospedale* and says she's not seasick but she has a problem; the nurse says come back tomorrow.
Jenny (loudly, for the seasick to hear): "But I think I have smallpox."
Nurse: "Sh-h-h. Come in here!"
And indeed two new large welts have erupted on Jenny's arm near her vaccination.
The nurse says her body is not fighting off the cowpox. The nurse tells Jenny she must fight it, but Jenny doesn't know quite how to fight the cowpox. She is remarkably cool in her affliction.

SEPTEMBER 2, 1968:

Lots of people seasick. Choppy sea.
Toward evening the sailors stretch guide ropes across the large rooms in expectation of gale winds. The ship is small and tosses.
There are dozens of "activities" scheduled "to keep everyone busy" and to prevent the dreaded "fornication" about which Carl was warned by the boat people when he went to arrange for us to get a reduced rate in exchange for a free show.

There are calisthenics, madrigal singing, language classes, poster making (poster making! O, *affiches* of the atelier of the Beaux Arts!), modern dance class, jazz, Carnival in Rio (no Night in Havana!), sketch class, music listening, films, chorus, hula dancing, bridge, chess, instrumentalists, "fertility rites" (don't believe it), skits, art lecture, folk dancing, poetry reading. And the many forums.

The forums are a horror of classroom behavior.
Today a complacent discussion of the Czech crisis.
Yet underneath something surges, as in the sea.
Those who attend the forums are in some way the "straightest," those studying to be schoolteachers, lawyers, diplomats, and yet . . .

I talk to a few of the students. They were at the Columbia Event. They keep their faith in their action and yet are brought down by its standstill. The youngest, Eric, is a friend of many of the New York pacifists and his mother a long-time member of the Women's Strike for Peace. He is a draft resister and sent back his draft card. He was on the planning committee of the Columbia affair. He talks with great assurance. He has no idea of the anarchist tendency of the revolution. He gets angry with me. He has no idea I admire him and fears that if he is bourgeois it is because it is his fate. Anarchism he finds "selfish," he is upset that I think he compromises. I mean to ask him to talk more about Columbia.
His friend says: "If you say what you really think they'll say 'Oh, that's just a commie, and then you can't influence anybody.' " Another, more sophisticated, has a background of the history of classical anarchy, but of the new anarchism he knows very little and of its strength he is unaware.

I sense a tendency:

The European students see the political scene

> subjectively: What can I do as a revolutionary? is their question.
> The Americans seem to be striving for an objective evaluation: What is this revolution about? is their question.

Only after the first question is answered can the second be understood.
The reverse is the illogical, but also the supra-logical.
To be it first and then to understand it.
Heresy to the rationalist, but at the crux of the new movement.

Tomorrow we are to do a forum on "Anarchy" and a performance of the *Mysteries*.
rehearsal in the theatre. I stay with Isha in the rolling cabin.

SEPTEMBER 3, 1968:

The panel decides to sit on the floor. The Riviera Lounge is much more crowded than ever before.
Julian speaks. Critique of Society. I speak. Steve Ben Israel speaks.
Paul Blackburn asks Julian if violence isn't necessary to make the new world.
Jenny speaks of nonviolence.
A young woman: What about the oppressed? Fanon. Is man basically good or bad?
Jenny commits an anarchist act.
Steve Ben Israel's pickle barrel:

> "If you put a fresh cucumber in a pickle barrel, you

get more pickles.
The same with nonviolence."

Then the discussion began to simmer and bubble.
A spirit of inquiry, then injury. Yelling. "They've got you by the balls," Julian shouts.
Talk about verbal violence.
It's off. Tremendous tension. A "white African" (his phrase) says he has been converted to pacifism by the actions of the pacifists, but he can't stand the word "shit."
Rufus points out how this is, in fact, racism.
Jenny commits a second anarchist act.
The room sweats, people grab at the microphone.
Everyone is awake.
The ship is politicized.
Two years ago a discussion of anarchism would have met with disdain; now it provokes serious considerations of anarchist economics, libertarian organization, and social alternatives.

At the end of the hour many still want to speak. The late session is concerned with "getting the apples to the city." Everyone picks up this phrase. A serious demand for a program is made, as though a precise economic production plan could be discussed in abstract here in mid-Atlantic, without reference to a time, a place, a city, a truck, and an apple orchard. But the questions are serious and only put to test the seriousness of the proposal. It asks in effect if the proposal works for practical purposes. They are asking to be convinced.

Conversation on the ship changes. They are talking about violence and nonviolence; about anarchism and authority.

First Living Theatre production on the seas.
The *Mid-Atlantic Mysteries*.

The first *Mysteries* for an American audience.
Captain and crew in a circle of chairs. Audience sitting on the waxed floor.
Gene at attention riveted to the keel.
Astonishment and respect and a certain discomfort come at me from the audience. A kind of "Oh, yeah?"
Sliding from disbelief into belief.
Afterwards the captain buys the company drinks. We are all disheveled from the Plague scene:
Captain di Marzo (Il Commandante): "I thank you, I have never seen anything like it before, and I will never see anything like it again."
To Julian he says: "I can understand the black flag, for that is not the flag of any country, but the red flag, that is the flag of a country . . ."

SEPTEMBER 7, 1968:

The ship has changed.
We've talked at the forums, on anarchism, on Paris/Mai, on student power, on nonviolence, on conscientious objection.
We've performed the *Mysteries*.
We've lived with them.
The staff members who guide the discussions are radicals.
The students want to be radical but are afraid.
The weather turns pleasant—sunbathers, swimmers on the deck. A lighter air.

SEPTEMBER 8, 1968:

An "ecumenical" service is designed.
Blaine Fisher, a Quaker minister. Some Scotch theologians.
Bread and wine on the table but not partaken of

". . . as a sign of our schism."

A sweet-voiced young woman sings

"He has touched your perfect body with his mind."

Gospel: The Good Samaritan, read by another young woman.
I read Psalm 104:

"There go the ships . . ."

And 121 responsively.
Even in the service, revolution is the key theme.

But Jenny's friend, Emily, says it is not typical of Americans.

(Yet she too is gone a season, and change is fast.)

Everyone is bated-breathing to see what America is.
The radio comes in, and sounds the same. Ads, bullshit, empty sounds.
But it simmers, it simmers.

There was a forum on American politics (the election) which was sparsely attended. The four who spoke as panel members for the four presidential "candidates" (McCarthy was added; Wallace found no supporter here, so a young man played his devil's advocate) spoke listlessly. No one could rouse the least enthusiasm.
The young McCarthy supporters, who were closest to some

feeling, were too brought down by McCarthy's political defeat. They can't shift to Humphrey or Nixon, and are just depressed.

Again and again the question is asked: But will it make any difference, whoever wins?

To my "know-nothing" view it seems that Nixon will be the next President—and he seems no worse or better than the others. The liveliness of a more "colorful man" like McCarthy or T. Kennedy would make little difference.

It was no better in the days of the much eulogized John K., with the Bay of Pigs, the missile crisis and atom tests.

The whole tone gets dull. The voices, monotonous. There is a mock election on the ship: signs read Vote, Vote, Vote, and DON'T VOTE in big letters. There seem to be anarchists on the poster committee.

"Thy banners make tyranny tremble."

The thought of the approach of the Statue of Liberty makes us all tremble. Everyone gets paranoid.

At midnight: Stoning of the Fish and Burial of the Pipes.

At 5:00 A.M., in the arc of the lights of the Verrazano Bridge, I unpack my valise on the upper deck and take out a black kerchief.

Carl climbs on a rail and affixes it as a banner to a rigging in the center of the ship.

By daybreak the decks are crowded and busy and none of the crew notices the unusual flag.

And so it came to pass that the *M/S Aurelia* sailed
Into New York Harbor
Under the Black Flag,
Not of piracy,
But of Anarchy.

SEPTEMBER 9, 1968:

The city, as the ship approaches, is enveloped in its smoke.
A red-hot sun shines among the peaks of the skyscrapers.
"It's a mountain," says Carl of the towers of the financial district.
But smoke billows out from the tops of the huge new buildings, and I think of the biblical word: the Fleshpots—for it smokes like a slaughterhouse.
The Europeans among us who see it for the first time are amazed, but because of what it has come to mean they are also horrified.
I didn't see the Statue of Liberty, but Julian points out the pyramidal roof of the Federal Courthouse.

When the ship docks, Saul Gottlieb comes into the cabin already crowded with friends using up the last there is. He is accompanied by a nervous lawyer and followed by Jim Gash of WNEW, into whose hand-held microphone I've talked for years, and though I've never spoken to him without his official equipment he seems like a friend.
The lawyer is panicky.
"This is what I'm here for. Be careful. They'll search every corner. Oh, God, there's a seed on the floor. Do you know what you can get for a seed?"
Everyone reassures him. Except Jenny Hecht, who likes to put the fear of the law in the lawyer.
Carl to Saul: Have you got the money? Saul: Yes.
Carl: Let me see the return-trip tickets. Saul: Here they are.
Sigh of relief. We don't want to land without certainty of our return.
Interviewer: "Are you ready for America?" I try to be cool and as polite as I can be and still say I'm scared.

Interviewer: "Do you think America is ready for you?" I try to talk hopefully (after all, I haven't even arrived), and I say that I was given a glimmer of hope by the students on the ship. But what one reads . . .

When he turns off the tape I tell him that I didn't want to say how scared shitless I am of the violent scene that's brewing.

Jim Gash has always been a very cool and neutral observer, an "objective reporter." But now he gets a very personal tone. I mean "involved." He says, "I was in Chicago"— and with a dramatically sinister change of tone: "America is *not* ready for you."

Like a threat.

I (naively): What do you think will happen to us?

He shakes his head a long time.

"I wish you luck." He leaves.

I had said that we came to speak peace—for whatever our saying it was worth (useful). I had said I hoped that we were not too late.

What kind of answer was that?

Was his head opened up for the first time in Chicago?

While we wait for the customs inspector, a policeman talks to Jenny: "You people ought to be put in padded cells—." Meanwhile our friends in hippie finery clamor outside the glass barrier, their laces and feathers dangling messy and glittery from their waving arms.

Television films our every move.

There was a long press conference. "Would you please define anarchism, Mr. and Mrs. Beck?"

And Jerry Tallmer—"I was at Chicago and Jerry Tallmer may just blow his vote to Richard Nixon or not vote at all." (Oh, Jerry, don't vote.)

And the dignified chap from NBC Television:

"How does it feel to be coming home?" while small Ben Howard gets into camera range and, standing behind our two self-conscious chairs, pees elegantly and at length on the deck, as we answer.

Ken Brown is there, from Yale. "It's very tight," he says, shaking his head, "very tight. You're needed. You've come just at the right time."
I ask if we're too late. He says not too late. But *he* wasn't at Chicago.

All these portents/omens/warnings.

At first the streets look the same, driving up the West Side Highway, only the new houses rising taller than the cliffs on the Palisades in New Jersey and some new box architecture seem to make an expected difference. Meanwhile, driving us up, David Stone talks about Chicago: "I was at Chicago," and we talk about the proclivity of the police for losing the public's sympathy by using techniques (violence) that are unnecessarily (and often dramatically) vicious.
It was the *raison d'être* of the provos of Amsterdam to make the police and the repressive society show its true colors. Now they call themselves ex-provos because their task in this respect has been accomplished.
They were not provocateurs to provoke the revolution; they were provoking the clarification that led to an understanding of why the revolution is necessary and on which direction it must focus.
And this is revolutionary work. In *Paradise Now* we call it the second rung of Revolutionary Action.
The destination must be made clear. North Pole/Crystallization.

Not only in Amsterdam but everywhere.

This is the time of the choosing of sides.
Corresponding to the gathering of the forces.

The rooms are the same. The television talks of local matters: a school strike, a fire in Harlem.
Rip Van Winkle wakes twenty years later and finds an unchanged world.
Wait. It looks the same but it's not the same.
The local matters hide: the conviction of Huey Newton:
The Black Panthers say: "We know what to do now."
Army trucks blown up in California.
School strike: a black leader, interviewed, angrily cries, "Racist."
A fire in Harlem: the burning ghetto.

Grandmother, crippled with arthritis, welcomes the new baby in her immaculate apartment on the edge of the black ghetto.
"Well," she says, "West End Avenue is what it was."
But the side streets are black.

More street lights, more cops on the street.
Looks the same. Isn't.

Above Union Square is Max's Kansas City, a restaurant where the "scene" is taking place and The Living Theatre actors come to meet their friends. Flower clothes and beads and funny hats obscure everyone.
Liveliness presides. Everyone is elated by the new town.
The Europeans shake their heads. It's all a false high.
Ask anyone. He tells you his theory. That it's bad, and false, frightening. Everyone's scared. Everyone talks all the time about being scared.

The sight is depressing, there is no grounding in reality: the reality is outside and represents the great opposing camp.
It becomes clear that Carl is right:
The energy is used up. Instead of revolution there is dressing up.
Genet says it in *The Maids:* "You've frittered away my frenzy."
The joyous permissiveness of the Revolution of Desire,
The intensity of the work of the Revolution to Supply Needs.
But the grim red rage of the *Enragés* inspires (though it frightens)
And the flowers only make us sad.

Walk on Broadway—more inhuman architecture replaces the old houses.

Tackiness: look of transience.
Decay of the illusions.

SEPTEMBER 10, 1968:

Elenore Lester, one of the first journalists ever to interview us, when we were doing an Evening of Bohemian Theatre at the Cherry Lane and she was working on the *Newark Star Ledger,* comes to make a story for the *New York Times.*
We tell old stories.

At Beverly Landau's Central Park West apartment/with a spectacular view of the city at night in its lights/there is a meeting of The Living Theatre, which is part party and part paranoia.

The lawyers (Bob Projansky, who came to the ship, and Jerry Ordover) distribute to all the actors the following paper, called "Legal Bulletin # 1":

LEGAL BULLETIN #1

1. You always have the constitutional right to consult your attorney. Insist on this right whenever you feel it is necessary.

2. Prior to arrest, you are never required to answer any police questions, except
   a) name
   b) address
   c) where you are going

and the policeman must have a good and lawful reason for asking even these questions.

3. Nobody has the right to search your home or your person (or your hotel room, tent, locker, suitcase, purse, car, etc.) unless
   a) you give him permission, or
   b) he has a search warrant, or
   c) you have been lawfully placed under

arrest before the search. Never let a policeman inside your door without a warrant unless you want him inside. NEVER FORCIBLY RESIST ARREST.

4. If arrested, give no information except name, address, age, birthplace, etc. Never discuss the facts of the charge against you; when questioned, refuse to answer, demand access to a telephone and call your attorney. Remember, anything you say can and will

be used against you, despite any promises the police may make to you.

5. A policeman may stop a car at any time and demand to see a license to drive and the auto registration. He may <u>not</u> arbitrarily search the car.

6. If you are arrested, call Bob Projansky at 212-228-7966 (day or night) and give your name, your local address, the charge against you, where you are being held and the telephone number. Mention The Living Theatre and the answering service will accept the charges.

Dated: September 10, 1968

JERALD ORDOVER
One Liberty Street
New York, New York
HAnover 5-7520

It is obvious that they, at least are frightened, Rufus is frightened. "I don't want to give my life for my country," he says. "Nor any country—." We were planning to travel across the country in our VW mini-buses. He will not travel in a small car across America because a black man is not safe on the roads in a car or in a train. He will travel only in a large chartered bus, because buses are not molested on the road by the police or others out to do mischief.
We decide to travel in a large chartered bus, plus two VWs.

Ken Brown describes New Haven with the accuracy with which he describes *The Brig* (as a prisoner): There are three kinds of police:

1. Campus police. On campus: plainclothes.
2. City police. Uniformed and plainclothes.
3. State police. Uniformed and plainclothes.

Every fourth person you see, says Ken, will be a cop.

Crazy paranoia is setting in.

Rubin Gorewitz, the Jewish mother of accountants, pleads with us to sign the compromise with the government on the so-called "taxes."* But we want to make clear that we believe we don't owe the government any money. He is determined that we sign the compromise to protect ourselves. Otherwise we are in constant danger.
We ask for tomorrow (time to think).
No, he wants to be sure before we open in New Haven.
He comes to dinner with us.
Dozens of pages/fine print/spread all over the table.
Julian signs holding Isha, sleeping in his arms.
We have agreed that if we ever make a great deal of money, we'll give some of it to the government. Julian is distressed. He doesn't want this to be taken to mean that we believe we owe any money to the government. I'm relieved that they can't suddenly pounce on us with unreasonable demands. I mean: I'm scared, especially if they're mad at us for something else—the way they prosecute supposed gangsters for supposed taxes and technicalities because they can't prove crimes against them. Why not politics, why not artists?
When it's getting worse you can't tell how much worse it's going to get, or how soon.
Perhaps I'm not objective enough. Paranoia's got me, too.

* In October of 1963 the Government closed The Living Theatre on Fourteenth Street claiming that the theatre owed a lot of money for admission and withholding taxes.

At midnight we go to Karl Bissinger's, where he has made a party for us.
Bessie Smith's too loud, so we settle Isha on a pillow on the floor in the hallway and sit in the stairwell talking to Mel Most.
Mel's anarchist projects:

> A month-long action in March '71 to commemorate:
> the hundredth anniversary of the Paris Commune,
> the fiftieth anniversary of the Kronstadt Rebellion,
> the thirty-fifth anniversary of the Barcelona Brigade.

Sure. I suggest border and Stock Exchange actions, as Jim Anderson and Mel Clay described them.

Jim Anderson suggests a protest against the existence of frontiers:

> Large groups of students, carrying no identity papers, gather at border points, mingle at the borderline, and dissolve the dividing line by their presence. They refuse (for the period of the demonstration) to betray their "nationality" by language or any other identification: thus for a short time the hostile differences between German/French, French/Italian etc., can be emblematically eliminated by an exemplary action.

Mel Clay suggests a show of solidarity of the youth against the international economic juggernaut:

> A disruption of all the great stock markets at a coordinated moment to give us hope that our forms of communication can overcome their ticker tape.

Mel Most shows us a rage-filled letter in *Rat* signed by Murray Bookchin with the sobriquet "Incontrollado," attacking Paul Goodman/because of the pacifism Paul attributes to the anarchist movement in a *New York Times* article called "The Black Flag of Anarchism."*

July 1967:
In an apartment in the Rue Troyon, in Paris, July 1967, right after Isha's birth, I was still confined to the house. Murray Bookchin came to see me and we talked all day: Murray refused to let us divide on the issue of violence; better to work on building up an anarchist program. He was full of grace and openness;
I wanted to talk about his justification of violence, and it was he who insisted that we talk instead of the anarchist student movement which he had come to Europe to observe. He said it was of far greater value for us to talk about consolidating the anarchist tendencies among the youth than to discuss ideological differences. I tried to insist that it was the pivotal question, but at his insistence we talked instead about the Revolution of Desire and Need, and about the students everywhere with their remarkable break-throughs and inspiring purity. His notions about ecology relate to some of the ideas of the Catholic Workers when they speak of the Green Revolution. He gives me two manuscripts: "Desire and Need,"† and

* "The Black Flag of Anarchism," by Paul Goodman, *New York Times Magazine,* July 14, 1968.
† "Desire and Need," by Murray Bookchin, *Anarchos I,* February 1968.

an article on ecology* by Lewis Herber, which he says is a pseudonym. I am impressed by his constructive ideas.

In Paris Murray insisted that the issue of violence should not divide us, but in this letter he insists that nonviolent anarchism is a paradox. He confuses nonviolent with nonrevolutionary. In his letter to *Rat,* Murray rages in Old-Left polemical style, as if Paul's nonviolent position betrayed the anarchist revolt.
But then again it's a year later.

Allen Ginsberg sends a message to Julian through Keith Lampke saying that he is anxious to discuss the stemming of the new wave of pro-violence.

Incidents: Cops stop a car:

> "You're Living Theatre. We know you, and we're one step ahead of you."

In the subway, cop to Carl Einhorn: "Okay, show me your papers."
People passing on the streets: "Welcome home, welcome back."

SEPTEMBER 11, 1968:

In one day: press: NBC Tonight Show, Channel 5 Television News, WBAI, *Newsweek,* Elenore Lester from the

* "Ecology and Revolutionary Thought," by Lewis Herber (Murray Bookchin), *Anarchos I,* February 1968, reprinted from *Anarchy* #69, November 1966.

Times, Bruce Grund from *Rat.*
Not because The Living Theatre needs all that publicity but because we can keep saying, "The Beautiful Nonviolent Anarchist Revolution."

We go down to Fourteenth Street to visit the old theatre. It has been sandblasted and looks awfully clean. We go upstairs in spite of a sign that says Moore-McCormack Lines, and open the door that was once the door to the back of the theatre. Wood-paneled offices, doors, a water cooler; nothing but the same old dank odor to remind us. On the other side is the door to the old office of the General Strike for Peace.
It's locked.
The door knob has been taken out. And through the round hole I see the back wall of the room we called the Strike Room. We built that wall of cinder blocks. We plastered it. Now on its dust a huge peace symbol is painted in black spray paint. As large as the wall, it fills the round space of the keyhole. It's crude. It's all that's left of our mark.

We walk down to Wooster Street noting what's changed and what's not changed.
The vile housing developments that undo the revolution.
The same laborers loading the bales onto trucks in the sweatshop district.
The Hare Krishna musicians and mendicants selling "Godhead."
The rottenness/the holiness/and the great beauty.

At Wooster Street there is the Performance Garage. Richard Schechner greets us in his environment theatre. Then *Newsweek* and WBAI and Channel 5 and *Ramparts* start asking us questions while 5 films the actors doing Lee's piece in the background.

Jenny is flipped out by the American scene:

"Evacuate the continent," she cries, waving her arms.

At NBC we drink coffee in the air-conditioned office of Johnny Carson's assistant on the Tonight Show. He talks of this and that in a chatty tone to report on our talents for the comedian.

It little matters to say, "The Beautiful Nonviolent Anarchist Revolution."

On the wall of his office, right there in the heart of it, is the poster of the protest against the Lincoln Center Film Festival. It's a mass of black paint—a blot—on which is printed:

"BLOT OUT BOURGEOIS CULTURE."

We talk about it. He says coolly that he thinks the festival will be stopped.

He attended "one of the meetings, but at that time no one knew exactly what was going to happen." I ask about occupying NBC-TV. He laughs and says it was tried "on the National Educational Network, with some success."

Elenore Lester talks for hours with Julian's mother and with us, about our childhoods, politics, stories. Into the night.

Larry Rivers bursts in with a motorcycle helmet. High, excited.

He has a play he must tell us about, a play in which all the actors are masturbating all the time. And the action stops when one of the actors comes. The lights go out except for a spotlight on the actor's orgasm. He calls the play *J-O*.

Bruce Grund comes to make a tape for *Rat*.

On the tape Larry is astonishingly unpoliticized. He's still concerned with the elections. He, who painted "The Russian Revolution"! But his heart, ah, his heart is in the best place.

The frivolity is not yet out of them, the New York artists. They don't believe that the revolution is a revolution.

SEPTEMBER 12, 1968:

We drive to New Haven. In the Hotel Duncan there's a television set in every room, on which are seen the electoral candidates and their crude play-acting.
Julian goes to set up the *Frankenstein* set in the Yale Theatre.
Gordon Rogoff comes to talk. Gordon is aware of everything that's happening. He feels weird inside this institution, knowing that it represents the epitome of what has to go, but he and Ken Brown and Arnold Weinstein seem to be trying for a free community inside the rigid structure. Gordon is close to his students; he believes they have already created the artistic community; he says they see it like it is. They do. But like everyone else they wonder where to turn.
The drama school classes are relaxed. No formality in the lectures.
In Gordon Rogoff's class there is open revolutionary spirit. No one questions the revolution. Yet they are all here in Yale, and they recognize their defect in being part of this institution.

SEPTEMBER 16, 1968:

In the *Mysteries* there is very much response. The long wait in the dark is filled with the sentimental preaching of a lady of religious bent. The audience's repartee is part dumb-bunny and part intelligent, as usual.*
The cast, not accustomed to understanding the language in which the spectator's words have been spoken, is shocked.
The "Street Songs" get enormous response. The chant increases into choral sound. The cries for revolution are drowned out in one huge drone.
First a few, then many students and other people from the audience come on stage. The circle becomes too wide for the stage to hold; an inner circle forms. The Chord becomes an incredible participation event. Everyone is elated by it.
Bob MacBeth, who played Ace in *The Apple,* comes with members of the New Lafayette Theatre: they occupy two rows in the orchestra and are the best-looking people in the house.
During the burial scene they sing a low, melancholy song:

> "It may be the last time."

It seems dramatic and appropriate. Everyone feels it.
They are enthusiastic afterwards.
We are much relieved. Julian was afraid they wouldn't like us, and Gwen Brown, who's making a television film of our

* *Time* Magazine, notorious for its inability to distinguish between the real and the unreal, reported in its review that the religious lady was a member of The Living Theatre company, and that we were "dishonest" when she denied being an actress. "Sitting at the back of the house, an actress—who dishonestly announces that she is not an actress—chides the titterers for their embarrassment" (*Time* Magazine, September 27, 1968).

United States tour, moving around with her ever present tape recorder, says they put us down at first, but got to like us as we went along. If that's so, it's the best praise.

SEPTEMBER 18, 1968:

Steve Schneck, from *Ramparts,* makes a tape, sitting with me out on the grass between the shady walks of the campus. He says that talking to members of The Living Theatre it's been interesting to be on the receiving end of the current distrust: "Are you the CIA man?" *Ramparts* has made much of the CIA presence on the campus, and now, of course, as a stranger among us . . . and asking questions with his tape recorder . . .
He says:

> "That's what the police state is.
> "We don't need a CIA man to feel his presence.
> "He is already among us by our distrust and suspicions."

That means: The paranoia is part of the game.
Planting paranoia is more effective than planting an underground agent.

Wherever he goes, if the talk goes to Chicago or anything like that/alas, too much is like that/, someone says or jokes, "Be careful, the petunias are bugged."
Sure, everyone believes my dressing room is bugged.
(I don't.)
What could they really learn from our talk?
That there's a rebellious spirit?

That people talk about ideas for more theatrical and less violent demonstrations?
That we (Living Theatre/friends) have small illegal quirks?
Why should anyone care what we say, when with the most irrelevant and uninteresting exceptions we say publicly what we say privately?

John Harriman of course does the paranoia thing. When I ask him how many Black Panthers he guesses there are in the United States, he writes a figure down on a piece of paper so as to avoid telling the "bug" what might be a secret. But his guess is a guess, and if someone has the exact figures they are either public knowledge or a secret, and if they are a secret, I'd doubt they are telling it to John. But he's wary, and tries to come on as if he knew more than he knows. But he's honest. He says: "That's a guess."

Yet for all that, we're sheltered here at Yale, among friends in a warm atmosphere. Warm weather, helpful people in the theatre, comfortable rooms near the theatre, a good scene with grass and trees for the children, plenty of encouragement for our work, respect.

In the classes the students ask questions to push us to the extreme of our position. They are testing us rather than questioning us. They are smart and want to challenge us. We say what we always say—"Change the world"—and they say "How?" and then we talk about it.
And after a while they come to the ultimate question:
Can it be done without violence?
And the need for evil, and man's basic goodness are questioned.
And we discuss revolution and Artaud.

At each performance of the *Mysteries,* the Chord grows larger and circles form within the circle, and students do all sorts of things in the Plague scene, as if it were *Paradise Now.*

SEPTEMBER 19, 1968:

On the opening night of *Antigone* a Greek woman who had spoken several times in class came up on the stage during the confrontation scene.
She was choked with feeling and spoke to the audience, incoherently, in a heavy accent. Something to the effect that we despoiled the Greek religion and the Greek theatre.
She was full of speechless feeling.
I lay silently on top of Polyneikes' body.
After a while she stopped and left the theatre.
I continued.
Her Antigone was more impassioned than mine.
She was full of bad feeling about us, but played out the meaning of the play. Outside in the lobby we could hear Dean Robert Brustein putting her down. Could hear her passionate replies.

After the performance we eat with Herman Krawitz, business manager of the Metropolitan Opera and a former schoolmate of Julian's at City College. He is the perfect liberal. He admires *Antigone* enormously. He feels ours is a fine technique. He approves our political message.
But he points out that it was the New York Film Festival which drew protests for their modest showing of even a Czech film, while the formal white-tie opening of the opera, with Rockefellers and the mayor and high society, was not troubled by the revolutionaries.

We told him how at the planning of the occupation of the Odéon there had been talk of occupying the Boulevard theatres and the Opéra and the Comédie Française, but that Julian had pointed out that to occupy the Comédie Française was to beat a dead horse.
He continues to believe that the Metropolitan Opera is invulnerable.
He says: "We are not a target . . . yet."
But he thinks the Metropolitan is too big to fall. Pride goeth.
His liberal mind is more troubled by the "problem" of hiring a fascist conductor, or a singer formerly sympathetic to the Nazi regime, when the standards must be primarily artistic.

SEPTEMBER 20, 1968:

Gordon Rogoff's class in directing. Political. They are revolutionary and unready. They feel the surge of change, but they look around their campus and their world, and they see a kind of imperturbable calm.

To speak of the revolution here—and everyone does—seems to break unnecessarily into the tranquility.
Seems to be making trouble where there seems to be peace.
Those who scream in pain are hidden away.
The suffering covered over. The containment is working well, the crushed spirits smile and move on in the gentle pattern. The scream of the factory worker is stifled under his hand guided to its inhuman work, and when the young soldiers leave the band plays, and the police directing traffic smile, the vial of Mace at their belts.
The Niceness is everywhere.

But the students don't believe it.
The silenced screams ring in their inner ears.

A young man from the SDS comes to discuss "local problems" to help us with the New Haven scene in *Paradise*. What are they protesting? The art gallery of the Mellons and their dirtied millions, and a road intended to cut through the city (for the good of the people!) which will cut Yale off from the ghetto by a ten-lane highway.
There are no war researches in Yale, they say.
There is no CIA control.
Protest the draft and the Vietnamese war. Support the action of the Columbia students.
They know it isn't enough, but the ivy's so thick you can't get through it.

SEPTEMBER 21, 1968:

We try to play the *Mysteries* to a house of free seats on Saturday afternoon. The actors went to the Hill Section ghetto to try to distribute free seats to people unlikely to visit the theatre.
But the seats are occupied sparsely and then only by the same students and friends, and two beautiful black children and four or five others.
And they all blow the Chord with us, but nothing is accomplished.
Of course, something is accomplished for whoever is reached in the audience, and one is as precious as one hundred.

But the break-through to the audience of the streets is not accomplished, and is yet far off.

SEPTEMBER 23, 1968:

On Rosh Hashana I go out to the elegant synagogue of Rabbi Bob Goldberg.
He had stopped Julian on the street and expressed his admiration. He talked about his arrests for the civil rights movement and how he has been trying to awaken his rich bourgeois congregation, however futile it seems.
The Synagogue of Miskan Israel, in Hampden, is built in the cool, well-lit, churchy style of the forties.
Rabbi Goldberg in flowing white robes* talks about anti-Semitism and racism, is much too defensive about the Jews. He objects to the disparagement by a current writer—(Trevor-Roper)—of the Old Testament as a book full of barbarism, and objects to Trevor-Roper's description of Roman and medieval Jewry as antisocial. And such apologies are unnecessary, for he admits the accusations are "true," but he objects that they are only part of the truth—i.e., the Scriptures are *also* humane and the ancient Jews *also* enlightened and sociable.
I wanted to tell him about Passaic County Jail, where I had only the Bible to read, and how I suffered at its barbarism. He speaks of the weaknesses of David, and I recall the Lord's command not to spare the infants of the conquered but to smash them against the walls. And those who took

* In 1970, in Paris, Rabbi Goldberg told me that he had discarded the use of his robes, as they are not essential in Jewish tradition.

pity on the conquered were commanded by the Lord to be
slain for their compassion.
Why defend such things? To what end deny them?

December, 1964:
Rabbi Friedman of Paterson came to my
cell in Passaic County Jail and said, "Read
the liturgy of the prayerbook, not the
Scriptures, for in the liturgy you will find
only compassion and goodness."
And, with the exception of the carnivorous
practices of the animal sacrifices, I found it
to be true. I borrowed a Siddur from the
strictest of the prison guards, a Russian Jew
whose father had been a general in the
Czar's army.

"Imagine," she boasted, "being a Jew
in Russia and going so far in those days
as to become a general." And I
imagined what kind of man he must
have been to be Jewish and Russian
and rise to such rank in the Czar's
army, and I shuddered.

She practiced his disciplines, and was
feared both by the inmates and by her
gentler Gentile fellow guards.
She lent me her prayer book.

She liked me because she thought I
was an "important" prisoner—(I had
"special privileges.")

I read the Siddur cover to cover; it was
loving and saved my spirit.
Rabbi Panitz heard my complaints and sent
me the works of Gurdjieff and Gandhi and

Avicenna,
and the *I Ching* and many other books of
the orientals to offset the pain of Our
Book.

I would happily hear explications to soften the pain at the "difficult passages," but I was offended at this intelligent man's apologies for our fathers' crimes.
The passage was the sacrifice of Isaac, and the rabbi made a touching implication that the draft system is a form of child sacrifice, as practiced both then and now. But I wondered if he includes the Israeli Army in this category of child sacrifice.

It is Rosh Hashana: in Brustein's class we talk of those things that we always talk about.
Brustein says afterwards, "Rabbi Malina would have been proud of you." But I think my father would have preferred that I had not missed the Yiskor service to attend the class. Or am I wrong?
Eric Gutkind says that my father gave up the trances of the Chassidic trip, which he loved, in order to do the practical work of helping the victims of our last great oppression.

Rosh Hashana, and we open *Frankenstein* at Yale in New Haven and Steven Ben Israel prays

"May the time not be distant, O Lord . . ."
as taps is played for the dead soldiers.

Rosh Hashana, and Cohn-Bendit is busted in the city of Frankfurt at the Book Fair for protesting a prize to an African who called out the police against protesting students.
A Jew busted in Germany in defense of the African blacks.
Blessed is he who is everyone's brother.

New Haven is pretty and the campus has that soft atmosphere that the rich prefer and know how to furnish.
We talk with Arnold Weinstein in the elegant setting of the professorial apartments at Yale; inside the pseudo-Gothic is the pseudo-secure. Everything that the parental lie told us was real is here. The quiet tastefulness, the serenity, the studious, book-lined atmosphere, the history of civilization. Not one false note: Look out at the lawns of the colleges, or up at Harkness Tower with its bells bonging away their predictable time. Look out. And Carl and Julian confront the revolution: their talk is not safe, because it is not academic: The immediate subject is the theatrical burning of the money. The real subject is the strategy of the revolution.
Carl became a revolutionary through Marxism. Julian became a revolutionary through faith.
I am gravely filled with doubts.

Remy Charlip brings us his children's books full of unflagging love.
Meanwhile, elsewhere: Jack Gelber's Cuban play opens to riots and injuries in New York.
Elsewhere: Vicky Rovere, once our co-worker in the General Strike for Peace, is busted in the Red Square in Moscow for distributing leaflets about the Czech invasion.
Elsewhere: The police are called into the University in Mexico City. There are already fifteen dead.*

* By early October there were sixty-six dead students in Mexico City, seventeen killed between September 19 and 24, and forty-nine killed on October 2. These are the official figures. Unofficial estimates put the dead at several hundred.

SEPTEMBER 25, 1968:

We rework the second scene of *Paradise,* which was once
called "Bolivia," and was later rewritten in August to deal
with Prague, to take place in Mexico City.
"What is to be done? Be the police. Be the rector of the
university and resign." Et cetera.
In a moment of grim humor, Julian calls this scene "the
horror city of the week."
I'm not sure that it hasn't always been so. That there haven't
always been scenes of violence in one place and then
another, throughout history.
But the media, mediating, draw us close together:
Can't ignore your brother's voice when it's screaming
in your ear.
The Machine is teaching us that Abel is indeed our brother,
as is Cain with his murderer's mark seeking wives in the
cities of the plain.
But Julian and Carl don't understand one another.
And my hope that we can do the work we want to do is
shaken.
The violent have no such arguments:
They see a man whom they believe to be their enemy, and
they annihilate him.
We begin without enemies, and when we confront the
oppressor . . . what then?
We begin to argue. Just when we need each other!
But we must, for our morality leads us to different actions.
And we are trying to differentiate right from wrong.
And we fall divided.
We need not. It is not necessary to argue or to come to
agreement, *even about actions.* It is only necessary to
confront violence with unremitting tenderness.

We need the true answer to violence.
And the true answer cannot be slaughter!
But we don't know the words to say. And violence grows around us. We saw it in Avignon.
And we will see it in America.

While the actors take down the *Frankenstein* set I have supper with Mack and Ann Gibbon.
They are tired and feel safe. They are surprised that I speak of the police with anxiety, that I fear I might be arrested.
"Arrested? For what?" asks Mack Gibbon, astonished.
"This is not a police state, you know!"
I show him Legal Bulletin #1 and bet him a nickel that we'll be arrested, though I haven't the slightest idea what for.
She sent Isha a big box of toys. He went to Yale with Julian.
As we leave she gives me the name of a senator in Illinois, Chuck Percy, married to the sister of a mutual friend, David Guyer:
"Just in case you get in trouble in Chicago . . ."

The Guyers are rich people. He worked or works for the United States Mission to the United Nations. When we picketed the building at the UN where his office is, he sent hot coffee down to Jonathan North, who was vigiling overnight in 15° temperature for the General Strike for Peace.

SEPTEMBER 26, 1968:

The opening of *Paradise Now* at the Yale Theatre: The students flooded the stage, unashamed and childlike. They scraped away at every veneer, they came close to being really present (and not yet Paradise, but the road to Paradise paved with . . .).

Nowhere in Europe was the participation so total, or the willingness so expressive. Yet the European students were far more political: This was the first time that no one sang the "Internationale."

There is a more ready, though less profound, commitment to the advocacy of anarchism as a principle: even spontaneous applause when we spell out ANARCHISM with our bodies. To the European student, anarchism may mean primarily a less rigid concept than the alternatives offered by the various factions of the Communist-Socialist Left. But the American students are not interested in the ramifications of the "New Left," which many of them regard as a kind of journalistic concept anyway. They rebel at the rigidity of the Communist-Maoist-Trotskyist ideologies. The word anarchism rings truer to them because of its libertarian connotations and its innate quality of being unhampered by "party line."*

There is too little realization of the orderliness and organization implied by the anarchist concept.

In the play we try to provide signposts: telling as much as we can.

The last scene of *Paradise* moves out into the street. The night is warm and pleasant, and I think how nice it is that here there is no one to disturb, as the students are used to the sound of merriment in the streets. The students ride on the shoulders of the actors, the actresses ride on the

* This was only six weeks after "Chicago." By 1970 this was no longer true. The American students began to feel strong political commitments, and six months later American youth was beginning to be more and more ideologically oriented.

shoulders of the students; the people move along York Street quietly and with the gentle elation that *Paradise* offers.
I'm tired, and decide to return to the dressing-room.
En route I encounter Bob Brustein. He hands me a yellow flower, and with a consoling embrace he says, rather laughingly, "Judith, I must tell you, I *hate* this play."
And we talked about that for a while. He feared that "this is a field left open to anything, even fascism."
He fears that given freedom the people will choose fascism.
Of course this is the fear that keeps the people from having their freedom.
And as we are talking about this, a member of the audience comes to us,* and bending down asks if I will sit up on his shoulders, and so I do, holding my yellow flower, and he walks with me toward the corner of York and Chapel.
From my vantage point I see the police car ahead; as we come nearer I see two police with Windy between them.

Windy is very young. A poet-adventurer, he has befriended the company. Everybody loves him.

Windy's body doubled down. I thought he had been hit, because of the contraction of his body as it folded between the two cops. Later I learned they had used Mace.
I said to the young man on whose shoulders I was riding, "Let me down, they're beating people up."
As I was lowered to the ground, the students surrounding the police car were saying, "No violence, no violence." And the police heard them. And then the students sang "America."
A cop pointed at Carl. I thought they might arrest him. I

* Tom Walker, a Yale student, who, two and a half years later, became a member of The Living Theatre in Brazil.

turned and said to two people who had been walking with us that I was afraid there would be a bad scene; I started back to the theatre.
As I reached the corner I saw Julian being escorted to the paddy wagon parked in the intersection at York and Chapel. There is a policeman on either side of Julian and another at the door of the wagon.
As I approach I see Pierre Devis inside the wagon.
Indicating Julian I say to the policeman:

"That's my husband; can I go with him?"

The policeman gestured to the wagon. I went inside, following Julian up the narrow steps.
Our two companions from the street had accompanied me to the wagon. "Get out of here," said the policeman to the bearded man with the colorful tunic.
"I'll take my clothes off," said our friend.
"Get in," said the cop.
Jenny came and entered the wagon uninvited.
The man in the colorful tunic introduced himself. He is Ira Cohen, who edits the magazine *GNAOUA* and is a poet and everybody's friend. His friend is Jill MacIntyre.
We are cheerful. Busted.
Eighteen days in the country and busted already.
Jenny reminds us that she had predicted we would be busted at the first performance of *Paradise Now*.
Cheerful, as always, in the high of getting busted.
The students raise their fingers in a V as we drive by.
Maybe it always happens that way because the commitment has already been made; because the fear of being busted no longer exists. Because there's nothing to do except what happens.

Booked by a polite cop, we are put in separate cells on a

small corridor. The policeman comes to the corridor and in a clear voice reads to us our "rights." A friendly matron asks lots of questions, not officially, but because as she says, "It isn't every day we get theatre people in here."
The warm night has turned cold.
We sit in our freezing cells in our *Paradise* costumes.
No bed. A wooden plank attached to the wall like a shelf.
Running water, controlled by a button, which when pushed releases one bowl of water and then stops, and not before, nor can the volume be controlled. A toilet in each cell.
Cement floor, metal walls, hexagonal bars, a door of bars with a large elaborate polished brass lock that is elaborately inscribed "Van Dorn Iron Works." After a while the matron comes with a pile of clothes that our friends brought from the dressing room.
One at a time we are let out of our cells to identify a piece of clothing. The matron then carefully searches the item, pockets and seams.
"If you've never been arrested," she says, "this may seem strange, but it's perfectly routine."
The clothes are lying on a medical examination table.
My *Antigone* costume is there, and the white corduroy pants that I wear in the Plague scene.
The corduroys are warmer but I choose the *Antigone* costume because the corduroys are not cool.
During the performance I had put the charred remains of two one-dollar bills into one of the pockets.
Merely as a souvenir—for a bookmark, perhaps.
The student who burned a hundred dollars had held up another hundred-dollar bill which he promised to send to Biafra. The large sum, which sent the chills down everyone's spine because beyond symbol lay wastefulness, was completely destroyed by the flames.
I returned to the cell dressed as Antigone, still freezing.

Jenny, not having her nose drops, spent the time choking and almost unable to breathe.
The matron searched the rest of the clothes / those we hadn't designated—including the white corduroys. The clothes were apparently taken hurriedly from the dressing-room racks and not sorted out as to who needed what/.
My cell was the last on the corridor, except for cell 10, where a sad black girl lay sleeping.
I saw the matron look through the pockets and replace the contents. She returned, held my white corduroys up in the corridor, and asked whose they were.
And I denied my own pants.
Because of the burned money.

We all try to sleep, Jenny snuffling and choking, all of us too cold to sleep. We joke. We talk. Jenny, Judith, and Jill in jail. Sounds like a children's book, says Jill; then Nona comes in costume, charged with breach of the peace.
Jenny, Judith, Jill, and Nona in jail.

At four-thirty, as dawn begins to appear behind the barred window, the lawyer, Bob Projansky, with a bail bondsman, and John Harriman and Saul and his bride Oda come and take us out. Charged with "indecent exposure," they tell us; and some of us charged with interfering with an officer, and with breach of the peace.
I am the only one who is charged with all three.

SEPTEMBER 27, 1968:

In the courtroom, one of those cluttered, confused court-rooms in a courthouse not yet "modernized" and coping with nineteenth-century architecture, not well made over. After long hassling a date for trial is set. Yom Kippur.

Those charged with indecent exposure are supposed to have breached one of the laws which fall into the category of "chastity laws" and must take a test for venereal disease. We are dispatched to the Health Department. Here, in a building in the modern concrete-and-glass-fortress style, we are greeted by a large sign warning us that this building is protected by dogs.

A nurse, who complains that we are ruining her weekend by all appearing in a bunch like this, takes blood for our Wassermans.

"I'm not allowed to take my clothes off without a Wasserman."

The local newspapers are full of weird stories about nude men chasing nude women out of the theatre.

At night there is a crowd at the door that can't be let in/; the stage and aisles and theatre are full.

There are chants of "Open the doors." Both from outside and inside.

Shari tries to get the audience to open the doors.

When Michele and Mary Mary touch the doors they are grabbed by the police. I retreat to the dressing room.

Rufus is the peacemaker. He pleads with the people not to open the doors.

He promises a free performance to those outside if they will retreat. He wants to prevent broken heads.

There is strong feeling in the company. What is right and what is wrong has gotten blurry. What is good and what is bad is no longer clear and simple. That's what happens on the spot.

The night before, it was Rufus who dissuaded the crowd

from following the police to the courthouse, where there would have been a scene of protest and, with an aroused group and an aroused police force, very possibly, broken heads.

Carl believes that if two hundred spectators had tried to open the doors the police would not have attacked. I feel otherwise. I argue that Rufus prevented violence both at the arrest and at the theatre.
The members of the company talk about it all the time.

This time is a revolutionary period just because we are so constantly put in this fix: Not only we, of course, but everyone is constantly forced to act on decisions based on difficult conscious moral judgments.

All of us are, by the nature of the times, put up against the line we have drawn, and if we stumble against it, we find ourselves retreating backward, and it's not a line, but a wall we're up against.

Michael is Lenore's husband: They are the sixth and seventh of the clan of Howard to be attached to the company of The Living Theatre. She is demure; he is energetic.
In the midst of our distress at the alienation of the black revolution from the pacifist revolution, Michael makes things worse.
I only saw him come to the dressing room, shaken, saying he'd done something wrong, and I asked him, in the midst of all the pressure, not to tell me about it, but to observe the play, to play only what made him feel good and secure. I should have been more patient with him and heard him out.

Later Jenny tells me, I hope inaccurately, that during the New Haven scene Michael said to a young angry black

activist, "It's more your fault than mine that you're not free." Everyone is appalled.
During the play someone arranges a meeting with Ronnie Johnson of the Hill Parents' Association, the activist black group in New Haven: He and some of the other members will meet with The Living Theatre and talk . . .
Tomorrow . . .

SEPTEMBER 28, 1968:

At the invitation of Werner Roder I come to the Divinity School to talk about the plays.
These students are quieter than the others; they dress more conservatively, they express themselves less vehemently: But they are closer, much closer to the revolution as we envisage it, because its basic principles are already accepted. Of course I've always been better able to speak to religious people than to anyone else. I feel easier with them, and I can be simpler with them, and not defensive.
They too are frightened, confused, willing to make compromises because they think the emergency of the times requires it. We talk about theatre only peripherally. No one who is serious is talking about anything other than the revolution . . . and the violence.
But they are full of peaceable love, and even in their fear they can accept the premises of peaceable love, and they don't challenge it.

We go from the divinity school to Dr. Roder's house, surrounded by flower gardens; and talk about it more deeply.

They are scared to death. Admitting the immorality of voting, they are going to vote out of fear.
The most radical of the young men allies his sympathies with the Black Panthers; he feels that the sooner the revolution "hits the fan," as he puts it, the less the bloodshed (the old argument for the use of the atom bomb). And because of this he proposes to vote for Wallace, as Wallace's election would be most likely to bring about the revolutionary situation.
Roder is horrified. For his part, however, he has not a much better choice: only to vote for Humphrey to prevent the danger of Wallace's election. Thus the two interact for compounded evil.
And they all believe me when I assure them that the real power—the uncorrupted power—lies in direct action, and not in electing men to wield corrupted
power; and though they believe me they can't believe me enough, and they say, "Yes, but . . ."
And "Yes, but . . ." is the doom of all the good people.

I go to talk with a group of first-year directing students while members of the company meet with some of the Hill Parents' Association. These black militants have a vigorous reputation in New Haven, and are much feared and respected at the same time. Their leadership has been harassed by the law and the police. Ronnie Johnson: They say he is articulate, intelligent, extreme, and beautiful. He puts us down for rousing up the audience and then not leading them into revolutionary action. He understandably objects to our not having opened the doors. He feels we deal with problems that we do not thoroughly understand. Of course that's true; mostly they say he puts us down for our concept of peaceful revolution. But withal he recognizes our good will and accepts our friendship. It is toward Rufus that the most severe criticism is leveled. "You are going to get your ass kicked," they say, implying or saying (I'm not sure, I wasn't there, and these are delicate matters to quote or misquote) that Rufus as a black and as a revolutionary is mistaken in his loyalties.

Rufus is not unmoved. He rages. He talks of leaving this land. He shakes with rage. He is torn and divided. He stalks up and down in his beautiful robes and says this and says that but finds no satisfaction.
It's real, this anguish, and there is no answer.

During this meeting John Harriman walks out of the theatre where the meeting is being held, quietly—for no one actually saw him leave—and without saying anything to anyone.
He is not seen again.
He leaves his room in the kind of disorder that leads one to believe he intended to return. Concern grows during the performance. Everyone repeats John's habitually paranoid statements: "They're out to get me," etc.

The company's rooms are locked up by the Taft Hotel on Chapel Street, till Saul can find the money in New York (on *erev* Yom Kippur) to cover the rent.

The performance is nervous.
Where is John?
Police and plainclothesmen chase Windy Simons through the building during the play. His parents are after him.
A paddy wagon is parked in front of the theatre during the last scene.
The actors stay inside the theatre at the end of the play.
We gather in the little vestibule of the Yale Theatre and kiss the audience good night. Since it is also the farewell

performance for New Haven, there is much warmth and sentiment.

I watch the audience leave from the windows above. They don't go home but mill around in front of the theatre, among the many policemen.

Till one of the police takes up his bull horn and announces that anyone who doesn't leave within ten minutes will be arrested.

SEPTEMBER 29, 1968:

Where is John Harriman? Gathering in corners people ask each other this question. There is speculation.

Another meeting of the Hill Parents and Ronnie Johnson with some of the actors and Julian. I stay with Isha.

Mark Rudd talks at Yale: Reports come to me of both meetings. Radical and violent.

We drive to New York amid talk of strikes: The teachers are on strike and the druggists threaten strikes and so do the longshoremen and the police and the firemen and the garbage collectors.

SEPTEMBER 30, 1968:

In the cool spectacular towers of CBS, Stan Koven interviews us so informally that we are surprised that there is a tape running. Somewhere halfway in the interview we realized that it was no longer conversation but a public statement.

The black cab driver says in response to a question about his political position: "I just want to be happy and whistle."
But then he admits that he foresees that things will get worse.
In fact: "There's going to be a bad time."
And then: "The sooner the better."
"Because when it gets bad enough, it's going to change."
He gets less happy and whistly as he talks.
He implies that he's going to vote for Wallace because he thinks it will hasten the revolution.
In Ratner's, Howard Judson of *Time* says that the current joke there is that "sixty-nine is the year the United States goes down."

Walking in the East Village, I see a very depressed mode, frantic and full of need. The ghetto children and the hippies mingle, and maybe some nights it's beautiful.

OCTOBER 1, 1968:

We drive to New Haven only to spend the day in the clutches of the law's delay in having the trial postponed.
Jenny, in pain from dental surgery, is flipped out by John Harriman's disappearance. Her paranoia about our presence in the United States reaches monumental proportions.
As I try to calm her, sitting on a bench on the New Haven Green, the fourteen-acre park between the college and the courthouse, a Yale student approaches us with great feeling.

He kneels on the path before us:
"I beg you," he pleads, "don't go to the southern states.
"What you say is so good and beautiful and there they will only misunderstand and misinterpret.
"And they will use violence. They will harm you.
"They will try to kill you."

Jenny cries out: "Why should we be brave, why should anyone be brave?
"I'm going back to Europe, to be one of the survivors."

She weeps. She says she believes John is dead and the rest of us in danger.
At lunch she raves. She makes predictions that shake her whole body.
She says she has had a vision of Julian assassinated.
It horrifies her to tell this and she keeps saying it over and over, listening to herself with horror.
If she had the energy she might be hysterical, but she is underweight and pale and weak.

We sit on the grass for a conference with the lawyer.
He tells us the charges against us.

OCTOBER 2, 1968:

On Yom Kippur night *Frankenstein* opens in Brooklyn.
There are forty policemen in the house. They hang around at the back of the auditorium and backstage. There are three squad cars parked outside.
The play goes well. The audience is friendly: They are friends.

I know many of the people in the house. We play the Marcel Proust game: the description of the ball at which after many years' absence he finds all his friends in what looks like old-age makeup. Greetings and recognition take place through the wall of change.
There's Jack Gelber, grim from the riot-torn opening and closing of his Cuban play.
And Jackson MacLow, his despair making more sense than ever.

> *1955:*
> Ecology. I hadn't even heard the word in 1955. We were on trial for refusing to take shelter during the first New York City civil defense drill.
> On the witness stand Jackson MacLow said that he had protested because the bomb tests were poisoning the air and that they had upset nature's balance by the destruction of the Van Allen Belt and other atrocities. Of course at that time such testimony was dismissed as nonsense and crank-philosophy. He might as well have been Galileo.

There's Allen Ginsberg, full of warmth.

After the performance there is a party on the stage of the opera house next door. There are Robert Lewis and Clive Barnes full of praises. They are sitting at a table loaded with champagne and Boris Karloff Frankenstein masks. A loud rock-and-roll band is playing.

Allen asks me to dance and we move with the music till we both drop.

Under the loud sound he repeats mantras while we make
hand signals like mudras, much as in *Paradise Now*.
When we sink exhausted to the ground, still signaling
mudras, he mentions his age. I tell him the table:

Allen Ginsberg.	June 3, 1926
Judith Malina.	June 4, 1926
Marilyn Monroe.	June 5, 1926

One of us is dead and two of us are dancing.

We go to the dressing room to smoke and talk.
What is to be done?
Allen was at Chicago and shares the despair of all who were
there. But it is his commitment to be joyous and therefore
optimistic: He is committed to being permanently high.

> /"What else can you do?" he says in a Jewish way
> when I mention his high./

And so he has to supply some hopeful advice:

The police, says Allen, must be confronted by something
that soothes them, cools them, and pleases them.
He knows only of the rhythmic chanting of the sound "Om"
as being able to fulfill these requirements.
Where it has been tried it has worked, and in Chicago it
worked where it was tried.
There are other mantras that would work, but they are
longer and hard to teach to large numbers of people.
Jackson expresses doubt that "Om" would dissuade a
policeman from using violence.

I feel there is something wanting in the way of political
action where there is Om and Om only.

> /Granting that Om can be All and that All is not part
> but all. I am thinking of the policeman's position./

"Will it put the cop uptight?" I ask.
Allen: "Never."
He describes the sound, how it rises from belly to head.
He pronounces it with the long "AUM" sound of its alternate spelling.
They turn the lights off in the dressing room. We talk softly in the dark for several hours.

About peace. The "peace movement." Despair.

> *1961:*
> When we were organizing the General Strike for Peace in 1961 we wrote to Martin Buber and asked him for his support. And he answered us that he was in sympathy with our action but that he could not lend us his support for such an undertaking because he feared "the enormous despair" that would result from its inevitable failure.*

Now we are in the twilight of that despair.
Not yet its darkest hours.
The Voice of Peace is weak and tiny.
Allen wants it to say "Om."

He chants, taking two tiny cymbals from his pocket. His

* Jerusalem 17.12.1961
Dear Miss Malina, Dear Mr. Beck,
Although I share the feelings that have engendered your plan, I cannot agree to it. It is utterly impossible for me to believe in the possibility of a General Strike. Even the man who conceived the idea of a General Strike, the French syndicalist Georges Sorel, thought it to be a "social myth" only, and I cannot share his opinion that myths like this have a positive value because of their vitalizing the masses. Moreover, he had in mind such a Strike in France only. I dread the enormous despair that must be the consequence of the inevitable failure.
Faithfully, Martin Buber

enthusiastic hands make an incredible percussion. His voice rises in a blissful song that carries him away.

For a few minutes our fear is silenced. Imagine crowds of blissful youths chanting like that and disarming all that is armed with weapons, sweeping away hostility with a happy sound.
It's hard to imagine.
Is the window closed? They can look in. No, the room is dark. No one can see us.

Jenny comes into the dark dressing room hysterical and desperate. She sits up on the high window sill, Allen below her.
She says: "John Harriman is dead, and I have seen Julian Beck in a vision, killed."
Allen in an urgent tone chants an appropriate phrase in Hindi. To dispel the vision, he says.
She continues frantic.
Allen reasons with her: "Since Julian isn't dead, and you see his death in your head, whatever may be in the future, right now he is dead in your head, therefore it is in your head that we must prevent his death." And he chants.

But he is not untroubled, not at ease.
Does he believe magic can save us?
Certainly reason seems to have failed, but what is called reason is not reason, and what has failed is not reason.

But "magic" seems like another form of the enormous despair. The times are desperate. Try everything. Magic. Allen says he will teach the company breathing and mantras.

We talk and smoke and chant in the dark dressing room. The talk goes around and around.

How to love-zap the cops.
How to prevent the despair from becoming hate.
How to make peace.
Of old friends in the peace movement who are collecting guns.
Of LeRoi Jones, who appears to Allen in a sexual dream:
And Allen sends him the dream and LeRoi responds with abuse and insult and fear and rejection.
But Allen tells it tenderly and without anger.
But some despair.
Of Burroughs and Genet, who marched with the students in Chicago.
Of Om.

In the cab home Allen questions the driver, "What do you think?"
The driver is black, verbal, intelligent. He is for peace. He is afraid but brave. He cites King and Malcolm. He says he thought of voting for Dick Gregory—Allen Ginsberg is wearing a Dick Gregory election button and shows it to him—but the driver feels that's futile.
"King and Malcolm," the driver says, "had this in common: they both talked about their theories at home without danger, but when they went abroad and told the people outside of America about America, they were killed as soon as they got back."
Jenny's fears.
As Allen leaves the cab he leans close to the driver and says sharply and loudly: "Aummmm."
The driver looks surprised and then breaks into a big smile and says, "Yeah."
"See," says Allen, turning to me, "it's a harmless sound."
I had objected that to say it to a stranger would put him uptight. But not with Allen's beatific look.

OCTOBER 4, 1968:

We drive to New Haven for the trial.
The judge is straight, neither good nor bad; he has a tired look.
We saw him last week dispose of a couple of unfortunates with cool dispatch; if not particularly merciful, he is at least not a wisecracking joker like so many municipal judges who soften the pain of their job for themselves by embittering the poor with their mockery.
Judge Alexander has a reputation as a good guy.
The prosecuting attorney is a pleasant young man who doesn't really have it in for us but presents his case to win it.
Our lawyer is nervous but well prepared and full of energy.
He has with him a smart woman lawyer named Catherine Roraback, who whispers to him during the trial but says very little herself, except once when she suggests that the whole thing be dropped.
Jenny and Jill and Nona are dismissed because the arresting officer can't identify them. John Laporta, a Yale student, and Bruce Birchall the English director, are dismissed.

Officer Sullivan is a young man who has been on the police force for fourteen months and has already made over three hundred arrests, according to his testimony. That must be almost one arrest a day.
He's nervous at first, but after a while he answers less formally. The big question seems to be whether or not Julian or Pierre was "exposed."
At first the officer says that my breasts were exposed.
Later that it was only my left breast, and then later that it was only accidental, and that charge is dropped.
Sullivan claims he saw Pierre's and Julian's genitals, and our witnesses describe the costumes of *Paradise* to refute this.

As for Ira and me, we are charged with interfering with an officer, and Sullivan describes how we "wedged" ourselves between him and the paddy wagon to prevent Julian's arrest.

Bob Brustein and Jules Feiffer testify about what they saw. A student named Philip Welch testifies about what he saw.

Julian is religious and somber on the stand, even when asked ridiculous questions about his awareness of his genitals; he maintains a cool superior air.
I try to be so direct and open that no one will disbelieve me—not that I have faith it will work, but I'd rather be straight.
Ira Cohen doesn't play it straight and it's plain to Julian and me and we regret it. Later Ira agrees.
Pierre Devis—being a French poet—can't understand the prosecutor's legal jargon and answers simply, though he is dressed defiantly in a white lace cassock. He laughs at them later and says, "They think I'm too stupid to cross-examine."

Finally, after a day of wasteful procedures, the judge, in order not to let us off completely, drops all the exposure charges and holds Ira and me for interfering with an officer, and fines us $100 each. We appeal because of my probation.*

* Probation: When The Living Theatre's building on Fourteenth Street was closed by the IRS in October 1963, the company refused to leave the building because they felt and still feel that the tax claim was unjustified. After three and a half days the actors were physically removed by federal police. For this action Julian and I were indicted and tried on eleven counts of "interfering with Federal Officers in the pursuit of their duty." The trial resulted in brief jail sentences (of thirty and sixty days) for contempt of court, and five-year sentences, suspended, with Probation.

The courtroom is lined with Yale students and a few professors. Werner Roder, Robert Brustein, Gordon Rogoff, Arnold Weinstein, Thomas Walker, the student who carried me on his shoulders to the arrest, Jules Feiffer /who happens to be in New Haven for the opening of his first play, *Little Murders*—on the stand he identifies himself as "cartoonist and playwright"/. This assemblage of intellectuals watches the "due process" with greater than usual interest, for it is the time of the Choosing of the Sides—and the validity of the court of law as an arena of action is on everyone's mind. And the "riots" that the police provoke among peaceful demonstrators, as opposed to scenes in which the police are provoked, is a burning question, especially to those who were not in Chicago, at the barricades, or in the scenes of action.

It is useful for them as they see the lie win over the truth, to reevaluate their meaning of law and order. Brustein had publicly criticized our behavior in the federal court at the time of The Living Theatre trial; now he saw how the sense of outrage is hard to control, himself angered at misconstruction of reality by the process of lie-and-uphold. It is useful for the hundreds of students who saw me walk peacefully into the wagon at the policeman's invitation.

> "That's my husband; can I go with him?" /Gesture of assent./ Entry./

It is useful to hear the story constructed differently into a fiction about resisting police; to see me fined and found guilty; to learn that the lie of the policeman always wins over plain-spoken truth in the court of law.
It is good that this can be demonstrated in a small, safe, and unimportant case, where there is no real suffering, but where the suffering of the thousands in the jails, in the

deathhouses, in front of the firing squads is emblematically carried on in all its shrieking horror under the banner of "In God We Trust."
Everywhere, bit by bit, swiftly and slowly, the sham of the old values is exposed.
In the time of the Choosing of Sides only the totally blind can turn away from the light.
It is shining in our eyes. Makes us blink. Light of Liberty.
But in her sinister hand she holds the book of laws. No one uses the word liberty.
It is useful, even without knowing it, to set an example.

When the policeman testified, Jules Feiffer whispered to me, leaning over the lawyer's desk, "Can't they see in his face (the cop's) that he's lying?" No, they can't . . . Yes, they can, but they are defending something they believe is important. Because people can't just "get away with such things." Only the caricaturist, who is most expert at drawing the lying face, the false look—he can see it.

Racing back to Brooklyn for the *Frankenstein* performance.

OCTOBER 5, 1968:

A woman from *Women's Wear Daily* asks: "What do you really think reality is?" An interview in an Indian restaurant. I answer, "Pass the curry." "No, really," she says.
At the theatre Jenny is torn with emotion. She feels conspiracy rising against her and us all. She rants and raves. Her teeth hurt; John's gone; and Steve is with another woman. All this adds up to an enormous sense of political persecution. It is a trap and a truth:

The trap: To confuse the personal trauma and the political scene.
The truth: To experience the binding link between the personal and the political life.

OCTOBER 6, 1968:

The notorious Chicago newspaper sends a pretty young woman to interview us at Ratner's.

During the *Frankenstein* performance there is a political rally next door (in the adjoining opera house theatre) for James Farmer. Their backstage is adjacent to ours: filled with bodyguards and plainclothesmen.
The elegantly dressed black cops mill around backstage, where Mahalia Jackson waits for her cue while Governor Rockefeller speaks.
I decide I'd rather not approach LeRoi Jones in the lobby, where he stands in lovely African dress, because I feel he'd rather not talk to me. Maybe I'm wrong.
On the steps to backstage I find Shelley Winters. She came for the rally, not for *Frankenstein,* and she frets because her car is not here.
"I'm gonna try and hitch a ride with the governor," she says. The bodyguards and the black chauffeur standing around the huge limousine parked in front of the stage door laugh at her. She holds my wrist "I'm going to start campaigning tomorrow for Humphrey. Oh, I'm so afraid of Wallace; it's so dangerous, I'm going to do everything I can."

The breath of fear. On us all.

OCTOBER 7, 1968:

Abbie Hoffman calls us at Allen Ginsberg's instigation.
Talks to Julian, who says he emanates great sweetness on the phone.
The Yippies have found the perfect style for courtrooms.
Total disrespect for the stodgy nonsense of the "men in power" and all their formal ways.
Their presidential Pig candidate keeps getting arrested.
They've been less successful with the police; the pig enrages them, and the cries of "Oink, oink" and "Pig, pig" move them to violence.
We plan to meet with Abbie.

At Sardi's, at the meeting of the Drama Desk, the old world still creeps along.
Henry Hewes introduces us with apologies for his bad review.
Echnaton talks poetically about the meaning of community and Rufus speaks with his vehemence, as the theatre critics munch their free lunch, asking occasional questions which are politely phrased, with slightly insulting implications.
The only lively moment concerns the protest over the ban on Grotowski's American visit.
Julian suggests that the actors and intellectuals take some more vigorous form of protest action than a note of protest to the State Department—say, a strike action—to voice their objection to the ban on the Peking Opera, the Berliner Ensemble, and the Grotowski Theatre Laboratory.
There are vigorous objections: The ban on Grotowski is part of the American government's unwholesome way of waging "cultural warfare." To express disapproval of the intervention in Czechoslovakia the State Department "punishes" the European socialist countries by withdrawing

support for cultural events—the fact that Grotowski's work may go beyond his country's political position is outside their interests. The Peking Opera and the Berliner Ensemble, on the other hand, are unwelcome in the United States because they specifically *do* support the politics of their respective countries.

I argue that at bottom it's the same thing: the theatres are banned because of their country's politics. Rosamund Gilder and the liberal theatre critics of the Drama Desk insist that the two cases can't be compared. A lady sitting next to Rosamund Gilder uses strong language. Then they all go back to the sleep of Sardi's.

All media come to us. A kind of terrible lionization. There is discussion in the company as to whether we should pose for a cover photo for *Newsweek*. The actors feel used and bought. We point out that we are always living on that money. That that's where it's always been at, but they are only realizing now what we have said all along—that the whole existence of The Living Theatre as a money institution is controlled by the money from the very beginning. It is painful to confront oneself in the money mirror. Pose for the monster, for the cover.
There is a photographer from the *Saturday Evening Post,* Joe Constantino, who used to be a ball player and has a VW bus furnished like a comfortable house.
He plans a cover photo, too

> /he has photographed the Pope/,
> of all the babies of The Living Theatre naked.

And a fold-out revealing the company in *Paradise* costumes. Sic transit gloria mundi.

OCTOBER 8, 1968:

We go to the New School to hear Krishnamurti.
Walk along the familiar streets, changed only by the large amount of colorful pseudo-hip stuff being sold in all the shops. Op art purples and oranges dominating the advertisements, the shop windows full of colorful trash, yellow and pale and black and hectic red, and people's clothes (the commonness of the far-out), and paper stick-ons of daisies in many pastel colors which people put on their cars. That's being hip. And the whole area is hip.

The New School is very hip.
And the people who go to hear Krishnamurti are very hip. Aren't we?
And Krishnamurti is very hip.

Skinny, elegant, conspicuously well groomed with an obviously poetic face, forced, exquisite posture. . .
Perfection of manners.
Perfection of language.
Appearance of great suffering.

Krishnamurti crosses to the center of the stage with broad steps. His listeners seem to gasp.

> *1964:*
> Stage on which I played Lope de Vega's *Sheepwell, Fuente Ovejuna,* and Cassandra in *Agamemnon* more than twenty years ago, when it was Piscator's Dramatic Workshop (site of my first steps).

And Krishnamurti sits there waiting for the audience to breathe more calmly. He is not listening for silence, but, being exemplary, is making a preparation. His hands rest at his sides, on the seat of the folding chair.

And he asks about the opposites.
He says that they breed time.
And out of time is born suffering.
And in a scholarly, philosophical way he proves that there is no time, and it follows that there is no suffering.

His listeners ask respectful questions.
He answers patiently, intelligently.
The impression he gives is that he is suffering more than any of us (because he is more aware) and is transcending his own suffering in an exemplary way and that he is indicating to us to do likewise.
Why does he ask us to accept death but not accept suffering?
He assures us that suffering can be transcended.
But while there is suffering I am of it.

We also ask, "How can we end human suffering?" and we think first about war and hunger and disease and hard labor.
What man can change for other men.
Krishnamurti tells us that we must alleviate our own suffering in order to be capable of aiding others.
Of course, the path is parallel or nothing.

Everything Krishnamurti says is true:
But by his emphasis he places the foreground incorrectly.

I have seen too many good people wasting
their lives seeking their pivotal center, searching
for inner peace, and suffering more and more
as they considered their middles.
And I've seen others carrying pails of shit away,
and bringing pails of apples, hiding army deserters,

night and day scheming and plotting and planning to break down the walls.
And their lives too, full of suffering and messed up with delusions, impurities, compromises, and the screaming inner agony rebelling at death.
But they did so much. That much.

> Buber: For man the world is twofold, because of the twofold nature of his being.

Man's redemption lies in his work in relation to others.
A lone human being is an incomplete glory.
We were made for each other.

On our night off we go to see Rochelle Owens' *Futz*. We were far enough into rehearsals of this play to have a good idea of what The Living Theatre's production would have been like. It would have been an unbearably obscene horror play about Cy Futz' love for Amanda, the pig—funny, but always terrifying under the funny part. They did it quite sexy and pretty, very lively, full of dance, but it made it all cheerful; it took out her politics.
Yet it surprised us how many techniques were being worked on in common with us: the whole cast on stage all the time, the reliance on physical relationships as *mise en scène*, certain significant looks—eye relationships—with the spectators.

At the doorway buttons are available, free, in a bin with a sign saying: "Take one." They read:

> FUTZ for President.

Thus they relate to the event that is current—in an abstract way—
Did it occur to them to support the Yippie campaign that has nominated a pig for President: at great cost and hardship, and broken heads in Chicago?

If they had at least said "Amanda for President."
The artists want to associate themselves with the high-minded tenets of revolutionary action/—Liberty, Equality, Fraternity/We Shall Overcome— /but they dare not be partisan.

OCTOBER 9, 1968:

After the opening of *Mysteries* we sit around in the dressing room of the Brooklyn Academy of Music with some of the Yippie people and Abbie Hoffman and Paul Krassner.
They talk about their pig; they urge us to register, despite our anarchist principles, because "if you don't register, you can't vote for the pig."
Paul Krassner shows his brand-new voter registration card.
Abbie says they've arrested ten pigs and Julian laments that they probably kill the prisoner pigs.
Abbie points out that their purpose is to win the election, declare victory, and eat the candidate.
There's no dissuading them.
So gently, all night in smoky dressing room, crouching on the floor, sitting on, at, under the dressing table shelf, we sit there, delicately touching on the subject of violence, joking about our differences, smiling, listening very carefully, trying to respect where the other is at, very cool, maybe ultimately despairing of each other's potential. Maybe not.
I'd rather promote greater concern with anarchist social possibilities (e.g. Abbie's book, *Fuck the System*).
Only in the long run, as friends, could we begin to hear each other through the din of the conflicting ideological jargons.

Their boldness is the primary step.
It teaches the young to leave themselves nothing to lose.
Krassner gets disgusted with me because I mention God

/as extant/.

"God!" he cries. "You mean GOD-god!?"
"Yes."
"But Biafra," he says, despairing.
"Auschwitz," I answer "and still GOD-God."
After that he's sour on me for the rest of the evening.

The talk, under the façade of idle chatter, is about "confrontation."

No one has any answers to it. I can't resist making my pacifist pitch; but I have no useful suggestion to make.

That demonstrations shall consist of something more than lots of demonstrators getting hit and wounded and broken heads.

After they threw money from the balcony of the Stock Exchange, bulletproof glass was placed all around the railing at the Exchange lest the money /as is so often the case/ be followed by bullets.
For a while the market was paralyzed by a few dollar bills fluttering over the great money hub of the universe, and what's come of it?
Bulletproof glass partitions.

And maybe a shaking of the foundations of the mythology of the impregnability of the Money Idol.

I quote Mel Clay's notion that one "must disrupt twenty leading stock exchanges all over the world at one identical moment, to show them we are everywhere—Tokyo, Mexico City . . ."

Abbie laughs at me: "We've got better ones than that . . ."

Some classy people from the *Saturday Evening Post* stand at the door of the dressing room (they are doing that picture story on us) and watch us silently.

John Harriman returns, as mysteriously as he left, to take Jenny away. She cries to be rescued from the United States.

OCTOBER 11, 1968:

The manager of the Brooklyn Academy, Harvey Lichtenstein, is a sympathetic cat. He likes The Living Theatre and tries to be humanly helpful with all our special problems.
He's worried about *Paradise*.
Fearful because of the New Haven bust.
He arranges a meeting with the police in the office of the commissioner of parks and public whateveritis.
August Hecksher, whose name rings for me romantic bells about the Hecksher Foundation, and that first play of which I saw a glimpsing moment

> *Long ago:*
> About gargoyles that spoke, gray in a green-blue-purple light, to a little girl in a pale dress.
> I was very young. I don't recall anything more.
> Later I asked my mother about it and she said it was at the Hecksher Foundation.

That lost blue night when the gargoyles
talked.
I imagine they talked about Hope in the
murky purple.
She listens, enchanted, the little girl I've
chased through the *Spook Sonata,* and the
Mysteries, and *Paradise.*

Hecksher's office is in the zoo, in the old Arsenal Building. The lawyers are there, and lots of other people: city people, Brooklyn Academy people, Radical Theatre Repertory* people, the commissioner, impeccable, looking far more high class than the rest of us.
And Inspector Fandell and Lieutenant Mulligan of the police force.
In the commissioner's office everyone is very, very polite. Julian politely asks for no police at all, at the site of *Paradise.* The far-out nature of this first request discredits him, I feel, but he is right:
First ask for what you really want, so that your position is understood; then talk on their terms.

Inspector Fandell: ". . . normal police detail adequate to police this type of affair. . ."
". . . What you do inside the theatre is not our concern, but. . ."
Commissioner Hecksher [interrupting]: "You mean you wouldn't make an arrest for excessive nudity?"

* Radical Theatre Repertory was organized by Saul Gottlieb to aid the many radical theaters in the United States to arrange tours and engagements at home and abroad. The purpose of the organization was to help in the revolutionary work of politicizing the public. It was RTR, through the tireless efforts of Saul Gottlieb, that brought The Living Theatre back to the United States and that managed the American tour. Saul died in January 1971 at the age of forty six.

Fandell: ". . . the law . . . You must be covered from the shoulders to some designated point on the thigh."
Heckshеr: "But then you should make arrests for miniskirts."
Fandell: "The law is not always obeyed to the letter. But that's the law. If you're dressed there's no violation if you walk out on the sidewalks."
Julian: "What would you call a violation of the law?"
Fandell: "Nudity, undress, loud singing, obstructing the street. . ."
Julian: "But arrests for such minor incidents can lead to much greater, more serious incidents. . ."
Fandell: "You'll have to grant us the ability to judge how to act. . ."
Julian: "I can't. . ."

It went on like that. I spoke in a much more conciliatory (finky) manner. And they appreciated it. As we said goodbye August Hecksher drew me slightly to one side of his decorated office. "I wish I could have heard you say more, you speak so well."
The reward of compromise is the praise of compromisers.

But where are we pushing them?
Up against a wall?
And what will they do when they get there?
Shoot.
Everyone knows that.

If the way of revolution is to be a way of peace, we have to bring them to the point of turning.
Not to the point of shooting.
And everyone who considers it deeply ends despairing.

At the zoo cafeteria with Saul we talk about the Paranoid World. We talk about John Harriman and his concept of constant imminent danger, in the face of which only some secret can save us.

No one thinks deeply enough.
Those who look far despair.
Those who have hope don't look far enough.

OCTOBER 13, 1968:

Rapid events. The fast tempo of New York. Everything's staccato. Four performances on the weekend: a *Mysteries* matinee, then a quick meal with some television people who want to make an awful program called "Critique." Then an *Antigone* performance; afterwards Philip Smith, whom I doted on fifteen years ago. Now he is placid in the changing times. He lives on Sixth Street, watching the hippie scene. "I hardly see them, they are friends of mine. I only see them."

Meanwhile, in all this action Isha takes her first steps alone.

Sunday morning the *Times* carries a long Sunday Magazine section article about us written sympathetically by Elenore Lester. Publicity equals containment: there's not much to do about that. It is not that one is bought, it is that one is categorized and thus contained.

It is Jenny's farewell performance in *Antigone*. It is not the tender parting it should be. She feels we hate her for splitting, but it is she who feels she is running away. We'll meet her again in Europe. It doesn't seem like such a long time.

There was an ugly scene at New York University, where the students occupied two buildings to protest the dismissal of James Hackett as Dean of Afro-American Affairs because he called the three major presidential candidates racist bastards. The rector said he would evacuate the building "by any necessary means"/i.e., the police/ but was dissuaded from sending the police in (to a group which had promised to resist if the police came in) because "a large crowd had gathered." So they were lured out by trickery. A message was sent in that Hackett could be Dean of Afro-American Affairs. The students, rejoicing, emptied the buildings.
Then they were told the rest of the conditions: that he could be called dean or counseler of whatever they wanted to *but* he could have no official or other connection with the university and could only use school facilities if he paid rent for any space he used.

The students were irate, abashed, but still a minority group in the uptown school and without support by the larger part of the student body. The black students had barricaded themselves into the student center, and their white supporters, the SDS students, barricaded themselves into the library across the lawn.

> This terrible separation: Surely the white students must have pleaded to join with their comrades. I would be curious to have heard the talk in which it was decided to take separate buildings, black and white.

But in between, among the cops, a large part of the student body cried, "Throw them out, throw them out," and I heard a radio interviewer /WINS, "All the news, all the time"/ question some of these hostile passive students who said in a growling tone: "They have no right to keep us from classes."

Some of the activist students come to us. They ask us to come to a demonstration in Washington Square tomorrow —especially to incur arrests. We explain that we are on probation. . . .
These choices are hard to make: there is so much to do, the strength is so limited. The call is so urgent, the dues are so high, the rewards are so great.

Carl, on a bad trip, visits the lights of Times Square; there the absurdity of the razzle-dazzle dispels the demonic flashes.
Above the square sits the devil with a pitchfork atop a huge thermometer rising along one side of the former Times Building, now replastered and marked in eerie blue light, "Allied Chemical." This thermometer changes colors constantly, red to violet. Below is the world, a frozen planet in the grip of a polar bear.
What do these mad symbols mean?
But he laughs at a three-dimensional postcard of Christ opening his eyes and closing them as one moves the card slowly. Veronica's postcard.
Dispeller of demons.
And to a movie, a silly Technicolor called *Viking Queen.* Always the same theme: how gentle loving people are driven by cruelty to despair of their gentle ways and become fierce and bloodthirsty. In this one, as in many recent films, it is a useless fierceness, for the gentle-turned-fierce lose their battles and die, and their people are wiped out—and yet the spectator is expected to admire their last-ditch bloodiness.

OCTOBER 14, 1968:

In a taxi past the teachers' strike demonstration at City Hall. The little park, venerable in protests, was filled with orderly lines of teachers and their signs, dignified and sometimes witty, but not very; not a fervent gathering like our demonstrations and without dramatic sense.

But I saw the Panthers for the first time, and they were impressive.

They patrolled, in groups of four and five, the outside periphery of the area the cops were patrolling. They wore armbands, berets, were dressed in dark shirts with a white strap from shoulder to waist. They walked with a dramatic bold step. When they passed the police they nodded curtly and politely, like cop to cop, but there was a certain disdain in the mock equality. One is struck by their romantic beauty rather than the incipient violence. Their presence is their challenge.

The N.Y.U. demonstration took place. No one was arrested; the attention of the city was directed not at the students' protest but elsewhere, at the teachers' strike.

No support, no fervor for Hackett or for the betrayal.

No victory. No gains.

The teachers' strike is one of those issues in which everybody's head gets twisted. Muddling of the issues, lack of clarity, are the problems.

There is side-taking of a curious kind.

The nonpolitical people say, "Open the schools, the children cannot be victimized by this dispute."

The political people side with the Ocean Hill–Brownsville Board because it is the side of decentralization, local control, and autonomy for the blacks.

The "liberals" side with the teachers' union, because it's a union and because they are liberal.
The liberal side, because of the dominant Jewish leadership and membership of the teachers,

> /My son, the teacher—teaching and Medicine, the ideals of all ambitious Jewish parents:
> "Well, we're the people of the Book, aren't we?"/

has become the "Jewish side."
And there's plenty of black-Jewish, Jewish-black hostility.
This hostility is not new. It's been there all the time, but the time of the Choosing of Sides is also the time of unmasking.
My dentist, who makes fun of my political activism, says to me /confidentially, after the chair, as if it were a great secret/:
"You go to jail for them, you fight for their civil rights, but don't you know they don't like us?"
I take it he means because we're white and I answer accordingly, but he contradicts me:
"No, no, they're anti-Semitic! They never liked us!"
And I answer accordingly, but he only hears his own fears.
His maid, his cleaning woman is black—and she told him!
He looks at me with sad eyes. He tries to signal me, "Believe me! Understand!" I understand that he feels himself the persecuted, he who narrowly escaped Hitler. The Jewish Refugee.

Suffering has only taught him how to suffer.

When will the whole punitive system and punitive theory be rejected as we awaken to the realization that suffering doesn't teach?

We open *Paradise* in Brooklyn on an overcrowded stage.
Confusion takes over and again and again we bring it back

to form and content. It seems about to overwhelm us. So far we have always been able to bring the audience back to the ascendant-ladder form of the play after the periods of chaos.

The ardent ones sit on the stage but don't perform: Abbie Hoffman in his political comedian's costume, Dave Dellinger in his square outfit.
Richard Schechner takes all his clothes off at the end of "I'm not allowed to take my clothes off" and bows to the audience's applause.

The American audience is more given to chanting and dancing and clapping than to discussion.
As to "confrontation," what is that?
You look a man in the eye and say,

> "I'm here, you're there. Now where are we?"

Few personally believe in love (altruism?) as a "force"; or in "truth"—aggressive, positive, ardent, victorious, revolutionary, creative.

Fear everywhere: of Hitler, of death, of cancer, of drowning, of beetles, of the Void.

The wilder pressures of New York. Right now we are somewhat "famous," at least for this week or this month, and everyone wants a piece of our talk, or presence, because for this week it's special, like a restaurant's dish served only on alternate Thursdays.

OCTOBER 15, 1968:

To WBAI, where Ross Wetzsteon and Sam Blazer talk with us for an hour. A note from the control room:

> Sam—the pot's gotta go—FCC and all that—
> DANGER.

They are nervous at WBAI.

To the *Liberation* office at Beekman Street to make a tape with Dave Dellinger. Here, in the heart of it, a great mess reigns, that confusion of which Steve Ben Israel makes a loving speech in *Paradise* when he tells the audience:

> "You see all this confusion?
> Well, you're going to see more and more of it.
> Everywhere, there is going to be this confusion.
> Now start to work out what you are going to do with it. What do *you* want to do with this confusion?"

There is Dave McReynolds running for Congress on the Peace and Freedom ticket, shaving around his natty beard, right at the door, because that's where the mirror hangs.
I wonder who's in A. J. Muste's old office. Same posters, new texts: No War, Feed the Poor. Do It Now.
I sit on Ralph Di Gia's desk as he fills an envelope with peace buttons for me to give away on our tour. That desk faced the other way that first morning, the first time I was in this office.

> *1955:*
> We gathered here/it was June, 1955/to prepare for the first protest against the city's compulsory civil defense drills. We were going to sit quietly (peacefully) in City Hall Park, and refuse to take shelter. That was

my first civil disobedience action—my first demonstration and my first bust. Ralph and Dorothy Day and Ammon Hennacy and A. J. Muste, and Jim Peck and Bayard Rustin. . . . The case (a long trial) later became *The State of New York vs. Rocco Parilli and 28 Others acting together,* after an innocent man who earned his living shining shoes in City Hall Park, and who was grabbed with us.

I sat on Ralph's desk as Bayard explained that it was important to carry placards because otherwise the press could identify your act with whatever they wished. "This way you caption your own picture." (Now he's working for the Humphrey campaign.) Jackson MacLow had called me up to ask if I would join this action. We canceled the performance of *Phèdre* that night because Jackson, who was playing Theramène, and I (Phèdre) were still in jail.

So quickly, in Proustian time, it is years later, and the civil rights movement is the black power movement, and the peace movement is the protest movement and A. J. Muste is dead and the office is in the same confusion.

Dave Dellinger at his desk seems still too young to take on the role of Elder Pacifist.
And yet he bears it, like a heavy load, with serious face, and courage. . . . As if he had always worn those old-fashioned suits as if they were the paternal "mantle."
Bringing with him the years in jail, the years of community building, the years of printing, the years of publishing, the

years of writing, the years of quiet, devoted work in this cluttered office.

We make a tape with Dave Dellinger and Keith Lampke. They were at Chicago, and they have a discouraged air, like all those who were at Chicago, except Allen, who is the only one with a concrete suggestion (Om). Dave Dellinger says where Om was used it worked. But he feared for the whole concept of confrontation because so many didn't say "Om" but "Oink, oink," to enrage the police. He is patient. He is inquisitive. He asks what we have to suggest.

He asks a lot about the theatre.

There is a somber, nostalgic tone as Dave recalls how in 1962 in a barn in New Jersey we made colorful signs for the first Times Square peace demonstration after the ban following the 1962 Times Square riot. How we had a kind of hopeful energy then.

From the heart of the peace movement to the evil eye of the beast: to the Channel 5 studios for the Merv Griffin Show.

Briefed briefly before the show, between the makeup room and the dressing room—"He'll ask you about this and that: be natural"—we follow Mr. and Mrs. Arthur Murray, a lovely lady trombonist, and a popular baseball star onto the artificial set, very artificially constructed to represent the studio where this is taking place.

The guests sit lined up in upholstered swivel chairs.

Merv sits at a desk like a teacher, with his intellectual interpolater beside him. New guests enter, audience applauds, Merv has questions typed next to his elbows. Who we are. What to ask, say, etc., plus what kind of answer he can expect.

Julian and I talk for more than ten minutes on the beautiful nonviolent anarchist revolution.

They write it proudly on their walls: "35 Million People

Watch This Show"—35 million people!
Merv asks: In your society (*sic!* to speak for it is to possess it) does anyone have to work?
We say they do not.
"That's very Biblical," says the intellectual at M.G.'s left hand. "Jesus said, 'Behold the lilies of the field. . . .' They don't work but God supplies them with their needs and their beauty."
M.G. was taken aback. Don't have to work!
And went on for the 35 million.

At Schechner's garage all the radical theatre groups meet and talk (Peter Schuman: "We must not be too esoteric.") and show films.

OCTOBER 20, 1968:

New York performances are hard. The pace is hard, the tempo is hard, the audience extends a hard challenge. They are cool and bold, but they talk in clichés. The dialogue in *Mysteries* and *Paradise* is limited. No one ever proposes anything serious.

New York Events: A drama class at Columbia full of radical students, as at Yale.
Joe Constantino takes the photograph for the *Saturday Evening Post* with all the children naked.
Dinner with Jack Kroll for a *Newsweek* story.

"The Up Against the Wall, Motherfuckers" attend a performance of *Paradise*. They scare us at first with their vehemence but we get to like each other. They wave their baby around screaming, "This is the revolution," in a very loud voice—and they're right and we get along together.

Four performances in two days on the weekend destroy us. Everyone is edgy and nervous.

An article in the Sunday *Times* by Eric Bentley called "I Reject The Living Theatre."
Among the many inaccurate things, he says that I called Senator Eugene McCarthy a murderer, quoting an article in *EVO* misquoting my angry response to the woman from *Women's Wear Daily* who was defending the liberal.
I pointed out that not only were we all murderers, but certainly any man who was running for the office of Commander in Chief of the United States Army shared the collective guilt.* The journalist defended him by saying that he wrote polite letters to all his campaign workers. I said a letter-writing murderer is the same as any other, and this is now cited (by an old friend and supporter, dean of American intellectual theatre writers) as if I were name-calling in a tone that beclouds the whole revolutionary rhetoric.
It is as though I would holler, "Oink, oink," to arouse a policeman.
Strange times.

The great question looms: Is our goal destruction or transformation?
In the instant it is always transformation, because in the instant we confront the man, we can't wish his destruction, only his transformation.

* By collective guilt I mean that each of us who has not found a way to stop the killing shares in the guilt, in the guilt of our human helplessness in the face of human violence.

But in the theory (clarification of the destination) there is a "system" to destroy/transform. This system is a structure consisting of men who are doing things that they themselves don't love or approve.

> /Soldiers, cops, legislators/saying,
> "But we have to! There is no other way."

Even the great opposing camp is not the enemy. It is the structure.

"Shall I come down and slap you?" asks a woman's voice in the balcony as Gene stands at attention in the opening scene of a matinee performance of the *Mysteries*.
The question is repeated several times. Shortly a well-dressed young lady comes out of the audience.
The people applaud her audacity.
She goes to Gene Gordon, and turns to the audience, one hand to her mouth in the traditional gesture of an "aside," and says to the audience, "This is an Elizabethan insult."
Then she tweaks his beard.
He doesn't move.
She tweaks his beard again, harder.
He doesn't move, she grimaces at the audience.
She does it a third time.
The audience is stony silent.
She looks at him as if questioning his humanity.
The she shoves him, quite hard.
He stumbles sideways, off balance; by staggering, he remains on his feet.
As he recovers his position, he swings his arm in an arc, and slaps her hard, on her downstage cheek.
Her glasses fly off onto the stage floor.
Gene regains his attention position.

She holds her face with her hands and quickly,
undramatically leaves the stage.
Audience silent.
In the silence someone/I think it may have been Mel
Most/says, "That wasn't very nonviolent."
No one counters the remark. It was said gently, not
terribly reproachfully, but reproachfully.
She comes back for her glasses. After adjusting them she
turns to the audience and asks: "Isn't there any man here
who will defend me?"
After a while a single spokesman for the audience quietly
says, "No." She leaves the stage.

Paradise is so rich in encounters that we are overwhelmed by them and play them out one after the other, each one on his trip with whatever his part of the action brings him.

Such challenges are rarer in the *Mysteries* and, taking place in this static opening scene, the woman's scene was moving and sad.
It was a superb didactic play, though a pessimistic one for the absolute nonviolent.
It was a lesson in provocation and response. Julian says he went to pieces.
He could hardly speak in the Brig Dollar poem.

Allen Ginsberg joins us at a table where a lady from the *Washington Post* is questioning us. He is the great mediator. She doesn't even notice how delicately he begins to question her. Gradually he gives her the capacity to question herself.

He stands in the house left aisle during *Paradise,* a stormy session. Paul Mann is there bellowing his protest. Rufus confronts him and they bellow at each other at top heat.

The actors one by one take on the confrontation with the acting teacher.
He is more experienced at arguing than they. But he is wrong and it shows all the time.
Paul Mann rails his way out of the building. Steve Ben Israel is railing with him. Mann speaks of Art, of Structure, of Theatre. Steve yells:
"Fuck Art, Fuck the Structure, Fuck the Theatre. . . ."
Paul Mann rages. Steve goes further:
"Fuck everything. Fuck everyone. Fuck your mother. . . ."
Paul Mann slaps Steve Ben Israel in the face.

The performance day, matinee and evening, framed in the slap.
This vehemence! This needed, urgent, screaming vehemence!
Not violence. This is not violence.
Nor is it *Ahimsa*. Nor *Satyagraha*.
What is this?

It says:
We are here to destroy the system.
We are here to destroy the great taboo.
We begin with the great taboo.

That's why the liveliest of the revolutionaries call themselves the Motherfuckers. Why Ed Sanders, the most sophisticated of the poets, called his magazine of the arts *Fuck You*.

Allen is gentle. A Polish rebbe, a friendly voice. Howls, "The asshole is holy."

A young man named Michel Hakim wants to burn $4,000 on the stage tomorrow. He feels that it will destroy that part of the "money system" which is in his control. I plead with him, but to no avail.

> He said: "I have a great present for you tomorrow," and I was suspicious of his tone: there was a naughtiness in it. And I cajoled him into telling me.

I take him to Allen Ginsberg, who is sitting in the corner of the dressing room holding the Indian instrument with which he makes music. I tell Allen—with Michel's agreement to discuss it with him—of the plan.
Allen reacts humanly. He takes Michel by the waist, buries his bearded face in Michel's belly, and says urgently, "No, no, don't burn it. Give it to me." Then, looking up at Michel, almost alarmed, he fingers his instrument, and without taking his alarmed eyes off Michel, sings, loud and hard, some Indian syllables. Then he stops and smiles and says in his friendly voice:
"That's to make those particular demons go away."
Then, returning to his rabbinical tone, he explains that he should not equate the destruction of his part of the money with the destruction of the money system.
When we leave, Michel seems content not to do it.
He wants to join The Living Theatre.

The police are on strike. They form an exemplary picket line at City Hall. Three abreast, bearing neatly painted placards that state their demands in a dignified manner, thousands of cops in plainclothes march slowly behind the wooden barricades marked "Police Line—Do Not Cross." A few uniformed police mind the demonstration, their backs turned to their picketing comrades.
They mean to show us how to demonstrate within the bounds of law and order.
So many strained faces among the men walking together.
Across the street, toward Beekman Street, a small, straggly group of young people shouting at the marchers, who maintain silence. They carry a large sign: "Get a *job!*"

The traffic is jammed, we stop at the traffic island near the young hecklers.
An officious man is following an irate police captain (uniformed) toward the young protesters. The police captain is shouting, "They're harassing those men!"

OCTOBER 21, 1968:

We meet with Allen to learn mantras. We sit in the upstairs dressing room of the Brooklyn Academy of Music. He writes out the syllables. Rufus learns them conscientiously. Some are somber, some are sprightly. The children sing and dance. Allen leads and we follow him. When he sings he is transported exactly like the Rabbonim.

> *1930s:*
> *Zimiris* (songs): Every Friday night after dinner my father, my mother, and I sang the melodious old Chassidic songs, to conclude the ritual Shabbos meal.

That gentle ecstasy of the Zaddikim, as intense, but so different from the jazz frenzy. In this fervor and this trance there is no lack of control, but rather the very intensity is brought on by the heightened control—which is not control but mastery of the ecstatic state.

He sings the great Sutra of Aviloki:

> Blessed be he who hears the cry of anguish.
> Blessed be he who turns back from Nirvana.
> Blessed is he who has chosen to be the last.

> He who is Kwan-yin, Merciful and Divine,
> Avilokiteshvara.

It zaps us all.
He wants us to develop chants for political/theatrical uses.

Before each mantra he describes its uses as though it were medicinal/therapeutic.
Someone tells us that Hubert Humphrey is about to appear and make a campaign speech on a neighborhood street corner.
It is decided to go there to chant among the people who have come to hear the Vice President ask to be made President.
Of the many beautiful mantras, the simple

> Om Sri Maitreya

a welcome to the new, the forthcoming Buddha, is decided on.
We sit and talk awhile, smoke a little.
Then quite suddenly Allen takes his instrument and begins to play the chords and then to chant.
As he does so we all take up our coats and our babies, as we sing, at first quite softly,

> Om Sri Maitreya,

and we move out of the building, past the puzzled door guard of the Brooklyn Academy, into the fine autumn day.
No one pays much attention to us as we make our way through the afternoon scene in Brooklyn.
Our voices rise as we walk, and as the chanting becomes more difficult (because of fatigue) it becomes stronger and louder.
At the designated corner there is a crowd waiting around a

platform set up for the occasion, covered with placards advertising the man, some bunting and flags, all against the ludicrous, imposing background of the Dime Savings Bank, which was built to resemble a Greco–Roman temple and has over elegant white marble columns.

It is amazing how little stir our presence causes. But then they are awaiting Shelley Winters and won't settle for Allen Ginsberg.

Humphrey is late. The crowd awaits him, but we have a date with the Motherfuckers and it seems to us that we can't stand up the Motherfuckers for a presidential candidate. We can't stand up the revolutionaries for the Vice President. So we chant our way back to the Brooklyn Academy.

Before they arrive we sit with Allen on the dark stage of the Academy of Music and he sings to us his settings for the *Songs of Innocence, The Gray Monk* and some other Blake. They are simple, complex, always passionate. He works with the poet's ear for the moment of readiness and then swings out into great feeling, but always after a reasonable preparation.

The Motherfuckers arrive in all their creative disorder. They are the most farfetched of the revolutionaries. They have no respect for anyone or anything when it comes to the authoritarian structure, but they have a remarkably tender-hearted concern for the real values.

There is to be a benefit for the Columbia University students' bail fund tomorrow at the Fillmore Theatre. The Motherfuckers have been barred from the Fillmore by its owner, Bill Graham. I don't know for what trouble, but they are angry with him in any case.

In his old movie house Graham presents big-name pop groups and the young hippies flock from uptown to see the groups in the heart of the hip environment, and he fills the theatre several times a week, at prices which exclude the community because few on the Lower East Side can afford them. An effort was made, they tell us, to persuade Bill Graham to let the community have the theatre once a week free, but after agreeing he reneged and wants to hear no more of it.

Now the Up Against the Wall Motherfuckers will be allowed inside for the Columbia benefit, and they ask us if we, when it is our turn to perform, will do the first scene of *Paradise Now,* ending with:

> "Enact the culture of New York . . .
> "Change it . . ."

They want to use this piece as an introduction to the occupation of the theatre, at which time they (the MFs) will take over and call for the theatre to be declared

> "liberated"

and demand that Bill Graham either

> 1) give it to them once a week
> 2) give it to them permanently
> 3) or remove them forcibly
>   that is
>   call the cops.

We agree to support their occupation somehow.

I, of course, as always, believe there will be an instant bust.

> It seems that for all my faith in people, I always think people will call the cops, perhaps because I think them more cowardly than they are, or at least more cowardly and afraid than malicious. I thought they'd call the police when we went out to chant mantras for

> Humphrey. I thought they'd call the police when we occupied the Odéon.

We will do the first scene of *Paradise,* and when we call on the people to create subcultures, and to change the culture, we will not oppose their using the opportunity directly.

At dinner we talk with Allen and two friends about
"*Que Faire?*"
What can be done?
The subject is always the same:

> How to make Peace the Revolution and the Revolution Peace.
> How to persuade the *Enragés* to use their ferocity positively.

Allen keeps talking of choral sound and rhythmic movement.
He says we do it in the love pile when the Om-like sound rises out of the bodies.
He says Bill Graham is a good guy and a friend of his.

In the *Paradise* performance, during the first rung, I am attacked on stage by a hostile group of men. It was during the chanting of "If I Could Turn You On"; the stage was very crowded; there was hardly any room to dance; when this group grabbed me in the middle of the crowd, I chanted to them and accepted their mocking advances with as graceful/as paradisial/responses as I was able to muster. But it was soon out of my hands. Beyond a certain point, I saw it happen: that they were no longer compassionate.

Then they begin to fight among each other, and in fighting to get at me they hurt me beyond my capacity to either yield or resist. Hundreds of people surround us but the crowd is oblivious.

I was no longer addressing them. They were only addressing each other and I was their quarry. They lost all sense of my existence. "Hold her!" one said to the other, as if I weren't there.

Because the victim doesn't overcome the cruelty of the attacker, the victim shares in the guilt.
This is the challenge to our human minds.
We are given the commandment to use what we have.
We have the means to overcome all the problems that beset us: the human problems, the physical problems, the elemental problems.

> That's why the poet-philosophers believe that we can overcome death.

But we defer this divine element, this power, we abnegate (to despair and fear, I suppose, but I'm not sure).
And instead comes blame, guilt, hatred, and the fear that there's no other way to deal with the Other than to shut off from him.

Boundless love may be unbearable.
Or so traumatic that no one can tell it.

Pierre Devis stumbles on the scene and rescues me from my tormenters. I collapse in the dressing room.
I'm too weak to play and I run out to ask Dorothy Shari to play the letter "R" for me in the spelling out of "PARADISE" and "ANARCHISM," and then I return to the dressing room and lie prone on some clothes that Beverly Landau donated to The Living Theatre while Wynn Chamberlain tells me about a movie he wants to make out of *Paradise Now*.

OCTOBER 22, 1968:

The Fillmore East is packed with young people for the Columbia benefit. The radical theatres all perform or are to perform. We arrive late, but in time to see the end of the Open Theatre's piece about assassination. Many speakers. I'm still sick from the adventure of the night before and send out a note that I'm too spaced to speak and I stay in the dressing room. The dressing room is full of pre-bust excitement, but Julian is sure there will be no bust. I go out again to watch Abbie Hoffman's comedy routine about his bust scenes.

The audience is raunchy and ebullient; they heckle incessantly, always on a human level.

There are the Motherfuckers in conflict with the uniformed Fillmore ushers. There are also two groups that move with them: a bunch of lively black kids eight to ten years old who panhandled during the money-burning scenes in *Paradise,* and a group of older men referred to alternately as the MF Adjunct or as "Winos for Freedom."

Perhaps this is the first attempt to organize the unorganizable skid row community since François Villon.

These latter make a lot of noise.

The first rung is hard to play amidst all the shouting. I hear it from the dressing room. The text lines are echoed in chorus for audibility.

> "Be the culture of New York. Change it."

And then the Motherfuckers agitated for and announced The Occupation of the Fillmore.

From then on there was a paradisial bedlam.

This is the third time I've seen this scene played and it always has this next action in common:
The summoning of the owner/director of the theatre to appear and play the villain.

Without the bearing or the illustrious name of Jean Vilar or Jean-Louis Barrault, the owner of the Fillmore East, Bill Graham, comes out onto the stage, as they did, for the confrontation in which he is cast in such an unpleasant role.
Soon Graham and Julian are facing each other inside a small circle across hand-held mikes on the stage.
The rest of the audience can't see a thing and is screaming or just milling about the stage and the aisles. I watch from the top of the stairway upstage that leads to the dressing rooms.
Graham says: "If you want this theatre you better go and get money and buy it."

He's driven to that! That's where the backlash comes in. That's not even his position, but he feels cornered, angry, overpowered and outnumbered. He talks hard.
Late into the night the negotiations with him go on.
Julian is right, he won't call the police.

Disorder prevails. Those who have not seen *Paradise* think the performance is over. Many of the groups that intended to perform leave.
Some of the groups go on, planning and staging on parts of the stage and unfurling banners while the confrontation goes on inside the circle.

The chaos is that chaos which Steve Ben Israel has been describing so well in *Paradise*. This is the pattern of the confusion of the future; use it to work out how you're going to handle the confusion as it becomes more prevalent. Some people are at ease in such confusion.

I watch from the crowded catwalk above the stage that leads to the dressing rooms.
During the stormy revolutionary debate I stay in the dressing room talking with Lee Baxandall, who is analyzing the proceedings with a Brechtian eye. I rant awhile.
At last Graham agrees, angrily and reluctantly, to give the Fillmore to the community free every Wednesday night.*

OCTOBER 23, 1968:

Richard Avedon asks us to be photographed.
After a few portraits he suggests that we do without clothes.
About ten members of the company are there.
It's an easy atmosphere and we are high and he plays a tape of Allen reciting a sutra and making his music while we move around.
Avedon talks about the revolution. He speaks with great belief of our revolution. Though still a young man he has photographed many power men, and one could imagine him as the great opposing camp. But his ingenuous gestures convince me completely.
He gets very excited. He says he's never taken pictures while stoned. His psychedelic Beatle photographs look down on us.

* He did not. Some people say there was one free night. Others say not even that. But it never was "Free Wednesdays."

On one side of the studio is the lit stage space. Chiwe romps in Michele's arms. We space out in the white light.
Avedon takes hundreds of pictures. We move around a long time. Three assistants move around him briskly and silently, adjusting the lights, handing him freshly loaded cameras, changing a lens, holding a cardboard shade in front of his lens, replaying the tape of Allen chanting.
Avedon says, "These should be the most beautiful pictures in the world."
Everyone on the streets greets us. No anonymity.

Barry Stavis stops to talk to us on our way to the New York Times Building.
We stop for coffee. He's burning for the revolution. I ask him what he thinks will happen. He says very directly, almost glibly, that the stock market will crash and then the forces of revolution will take over. He feels himself aggressively involved.

When we left America everyone thought it a kind of humorous exaggeration when we said in answer to questions about our theatre's aims: "To bring about the revolution." Now this word is on everyone's tongue. The luncheonettes are full of people talking about the revolution.

At an interview in the Times Building with the Toyko *Shimbun* correspondent, the present reality seems far away; he alone speaks neither of the revolution nor of The Living Theatre: "Tell me about your theatre," is his only question and "Ah, yes," is repeatedly his only response. A miniskirted Japanese woman with an intelligent face snaps dozens of photos as Julian talks.
In the hallway of the Times Building the correspondent for *Corriere della Sera* stops us: "I want to do a story."

Only Joe Chaikin hasn't come to see our work. He is spending his time with the draft resisters. He's become a counselor for resisters and his days and nights are spent in this difficult and dangerous work.

OCTOBER 24, 1968:

The Cloisters:

The Unicorn of the Cluny is about love and its metaphysical states.
The Unicorn at the Cloisters is about the hunt and the capture.

New York City:
Richard Schechner has put the *Bacchae* in a garage, called it *Dionysus in 69,* built a scaffolding to hold an audience in a new arrangement.
His players have a beautiful soft tone.
The flic-flac of the classical and the jargon works, bridges the space between William Finley and the god *Dionysus.*

OCTOBER 25, 1968:

A company meeting.
It's scheduled to be held in the quarters of the Bread and Puppet Players. They work in the former Second Avenue Courthouse; I recall being arraigned there, but I can't remember on what occasion or for which action. No one is

there but a sign on the door directs us to a nearby East Side cellar.
An insane crush among the cockroaches on the straw mats covering the cellar floor. The children, Isha and Chiwe, play in the hammock as the company plans its transportation arrangements.
A collection is taken up among the actors for the Motherfuckers, some of whom live in this cellar.

At night on Eighth Street to buy Buber's *Tales of the Hasidim* for my nephew, Clifford Beck for his Bar Mitzvah. The street is filled with tourists, actors, students, media workers, liberals. But the atmosphere is not very different from that created by the nightly influx of fat businessmen who came to the Nut Club to see the life of Greenwich Village in the 1940s. But nowadays they aren't so drunk and this makes them a little gentler.

In our room in the Towers Hotel Elenore Lester tries to cut a tape about communities, but Isha, restless from her long day downtown and uptown, and the New York tempo, won't let us. We keep trying, but Isha cries, the machine won't work, and I get a migraine headache.

Carl goes uptown to see LeRoi Jones's play.
At the door he is told he can't come in. The man at the door is neither friendly nor unfriendly.

> "You know why, don't you?"
> "Sure," says Carl.
> "Okay," says the man at the door.

He is more friendly now that he sees that Carl understands where it's at.
The New Harlem.

OCTOBER 26, 1968:

At Clifford's Bar Mitzvah in the modernistic Lake Success Temple all is peace.
I have often given peace buttons to Julian's very, very straight family, and I once rather defiantly pressed the family to wear them. Word got around and here people ask me for a button "for my son" or "my daughter." I give them out, but pleasantly insist that they wear them then and there.
A lot of talk starts, but soon ends in frivolity—after all, it's a family get-together.
A young waiter with freckles and a stub nose makes a peace sign with his fingers behind the heads of the guests. Sidles up:

> "Got a button for me, baby?"
> Breaking the white-glove barrier.

Dick Schechner makes a long tape in the Towers room. We're tired and stoned and relaxed. Who knows what we said?

We move out of the Towers Hotel to West End Avenue. Farewell, Brookyln.

A lovely young woman named Moon comes to watch over Isha while we work.

OCTOBER 27, 1968:

We told CBS we didn't have time to do an interview and also a filming of the Plague scene and Brig Dollar. So they said they'd send a car.

Early in the morning a pretty blonde comes in a taxi to take us to the studio.
The show is called Camera 3. I was an extra on it long ago for a program called "Organization Man." The narrator, James Macandrew, remembers it (not me, of course; the show.)
Interviewed by Jack Kroll, who talks quite intelligently and coolly with us, through all the retakes and make-up adjustments and somebody waving cards saying "One Minute," "One-Half minute."
While the company arrives to rehearse the Brig Dollar Julian and I go to Finley Schaef's church in the village to talk about anarchy and revolution. The church is plain, filled with shabby and pretty revolutionary types and many old friends. Here too Karl Bissinger busies himself with the work of the Peace Center. And here too is the heart of the resistance movement, with its young heroes, the deserters and the nonregistrants.
When I want a few moments of privacy before the lecture Karl takes me into the Peace Center, where a gaunt, handsome youth gets paranoid. "Not here!" he says in an urgent voice out of the movies. And he leads me down to the bowling alley, where mattresses and personal belongings of a sparse utilitarian kind (like the contents of sailors' duffel bags with a few sentimental effects) are scattered around.

Here they are, already in the cellars, and it's only 1968.

The young man talks nervously about hiding, about amphetamine, about the police.
That's what people talk about in New York City.

We came down from CBS. They gave us a chauffeured car. The pretty blonde leads us along the studio maze, and there's this great Lincoln with push-button windows and a man, a slightly black man, in a uniform and a chauffeur's hat, and he opens and closes the doors.

We arrive in this thing at the little church where the roughly made poster—mimeographed—announces our talk.

Julian talks first. He tells the story. What about the Beautiful Nonviolent Anarchist Revolution?

The same questions. Hipper. Nearer actuality. These people are in on the problem. Paul Krassner asks Julian about what to say to the Vietnamese peasant whose village is attacked, and Julian shocks everyone by recommending surrender, along with dedication to another battle, the battle for, not another form of government, but a totally revolutionary situation.

Julian himself is surprised to hear himself say this.

My only bother with it is that it can't gain support. And yet, if it were the truth, if it were *Ahimsa,* the love force, and *Satyagraha,* the way of truth . . . it would not be surrender.

Now the word "deserter," with its former connotation of unfulfilled duty and villainy has become a proud word. And the word "black," which in the days when one politely said "colored" was a word of put-down, has become dignified and beautiful. If surrender meant to enter into battle, as deserter means to desert what is rotten, and as black means beautiful and soul-full . . . If surrender means give in not as in military jargon, but as a love act, then surrender is the opposite of attack.

If attack is violence, annihilation, destruction, hatred, then its opposite . . . but you don't call that surrender, you call that *Ahimsa* . . .

I am thinking about this when Julian says that shit is holy and a fervent young man with a crew cut and burning eyes stands up. He has been watching for this moment, and he says, making a blessing over Julian's head, "May God forgive you for using such language in his place of worship." And he steps up to the pulpit and with great vigor harangues for the Lord in the pithy vocabulary of Jehovah's Witnesses. He speaks of the last days, and he asks the listeners, who have now become a congregation, "Where are you?" and a smart aleck asks, "Where are you?" and he says, "Don't you worry about me. I'm right where the good Lord wants me," and he points up and down at his churchly surroundings.

He talks a long while and then he sits down.

There are more questions. And "Why did you come in a limousine?" Followed by talk about the dangers, folly, and necessity of working inside the system to destroy it—about when it's finky and when it's not.

Should one—how (and if ever)—talk about the Revolution on TV?

Or refuse ever to look out of CBS's eye and speak out of their loudspeakers?

And if so, when?

And if so, how, how much, under what conditions?

The contract says that the performers agree to do nothing in public or private that might offend or embarrass the network or any of its sponsors. What kind of shit is that? We talk about that.

We talk about how to make it work. The younger ones talk about communities and building the post-revolutionary world. The older ones talk about the difficulties of destroying the old structure.

Afterwards we sit in the Peace Center and eat chopped-egg sandwiches among the cockroaches and talk of the deaths of A. J. Muste and Matthew Ready Goodman, the old pacifist and the young man who burned his draft card; and the frivolity of the kids who use the word revolution to mean loud music and lots of dope vanishes into the church cellar with the rows of messy mattresses along the polished lanes.

The blonde guide from CBS finds us and asks for one of the humorous peace buttons and talks with us, and we talk with Karl Bissinger, who works with saintly modesty at the hardest work, and with a couple of young people who are in the heart of it, and who talk only straight like the best young people do today.

Back in the CBS studios we film the Brig Dollar and the Plague scene with an invited audience that sits on specially constructed bleachers. They are friendly and play vigorous participation scenes.

When I die in the Plague a woman sobs over my body, dropping hot tears on my sweaty face.

In the great media and in the cellar of the poor church they are talking about the revolution.
Some of them know what they mean when they say it.
And most of them don't.
While the ads, their antennae out for new jargon, cry, "Revolution!" In cars, cosmetics, clothes, in blazing psychedelic colors, they proclaim the far-out freedom, in refrigerators and finery and furs.

And we're balancing: life against death.
Everybody's telling the whole truth. Even the lies carefully formed and labeled "This is a lie" tell the truth. Nobody's fooled.
But everybody's afraid.

OCTOBER 29, 1968:

Two performances at Stony Brook, a university reputed to be far-out because there was a big pot-bust scandal and much protest about it.
But they are more smart aleck than far-out, more sarcastic than revolutionary.

Maybe that's the crucial difference.
Those who mean what we mean by the word revolution often have a kind of straight simplicity, a lack of that sophisticated irony that was so "in" in the 1940s.
The most advanced are the childish, the beatific, with the openness that is the beauty of the moronic, the mentally retarded; yes, yes, the mentally retarded who have a sweetness almost incompatible with the loss of innocence.
The loss of innocence.
The Edenic punishment.

On the other hand, there are the violent/sweet/very sarcastic ones of the revolution-for-the-hell-of-it group, who speak in a very sophisticated mode under the cover of naïveté, crassness, and common speech.
The Yippies and the Motherfuckers who are seriously exploring the frontiers of irony.
The pig for president, the scorn-alls.
By inversion they've taken humor to its breaking point and turned the cleverness into a swinging nihilism.
These are always saying they are violent and coming on peaceful.

These are all poets.

But at Stony Brook the students made hotheaded speeches about marijuana but had nothing to say about Bolivia or

cells, or life, for that matter. The legalization of their kicks was their "revolution." And that "revolution" will be lost as soon as it is won.
And their now illegal "kicks" will soon be packaged and marketed and programmed by Liggett & Myers.
As for us, they didn't really see us. We performed in the gym, and the ensuing confusion of areas of actions was not always paradisial.
But there were a few who heard us, and we heard them, and as long as there's one, I shouldn't complain.

We stayed with an English professor and his wife and son in a fine house in the country with a fine piece of woods behind it, and a large dog, and a violent Lichtenstein on the wall. A cartoon of a woman shooting a gun saying Baaam!!!! When I compared it to Cathy Berberian's oil painting of Mussolini on a horse she took it down

/temporarily, only not to offend me/.

He teaches a course on dramatic structure.
He asks Julian whether there is "any structure at all" to Living Theatre plays.
We talk of many things at lunch and breakfast but never mention the plays, which they obviously hate, and they haven't the slightest clue as to where we are at.
Nor can I give them any.

OCTOBER 31, 1968:

We drive to Orient Point, at the end of Long Island, to take the ferry to New London and drive on to Boston. The tiny diner at the ferry port is empty and off-season, but the fat counterman blurts out, "Hey, weren't you on the Merv Griffin Show?" His revolving book tray is crammed with rightist paperbacks full of hawkism and the hypocritical prudery that places them next to the sadistic novels that share the rack.

We arrive in Boston and go with Isha straight to a press conference.

The Kresge Auditorium! Years and years ago, when this building was new and famous, Julian and I drove out especially to visit this paragon of architecture by Saarinen. And at that time it was impressive, but now there is only this tricky shell of a pseudo-technological exterior housing a hall inadequate to anything more than a short lecture. But the seats are painted in alternating pastel colors and that little detail impressed us and we used that pattern for The Living Theatre when we constructed it with our careful labor on Fourteenth Street; now only the clay feet are left.

The press conference is in a new building across from the Kresge Auditorium, and this building is a student center and here a remarkable event is taking place.

A huge Dayglow-painted sign is stretched across the front of the modernistic building bearing the word SANCTUARY.

Inside is a young man named Mike O'Connell. He was a soldier and by a clarification of conscience decided to be a deserter.

"Deserter," this now ennobled word!

Full of calumny when it meant the desertion of vows, of loyalties, of comrades and cause.

Full of honor now to mean deserting the forces of evil, deserting the war cause, the hatred, the betrayers. And he asked the students of M.I.T. to give him sanctuary, and they took him in and with their persons they surround him.

Here is an air of great events. The main hall is filled with hundreds of students, blankets spread on the floor, the walls covered with posters and scrawls of advice.

> "If busted, call——," and the student center phone number.

People taking turns at a microphone all have their say, or read a newspaper item or give useful or useless advice.
The atmosphere is revolution.
They expect the bust at any moment.
The plan is nonviolent.
They plan to surround the one they are protecting with their bodies, but to use no force. Only to interpose themselves in some poetic manner that will speak to the police. They mean to embrace him and to be wrested from him and be arrested for being one with him. They are bright-eyed with revolutionary fervor. They are bright-eyed with sleeplessness. Every few hours there is a "scare" and they all gird themselves for the event and gather and sing, tightly packed around this young man.
The entrances, roof, stairways are ringed with students with walkie-talkies to warn of the approaching fuzz. An elaborate poster, larger than all the others, reads in ornate script:

> "Sorry, no Acid, no Pot"

and underneath, in smaller print:

> "Friendly Fuzz Welcome"

Though it is beautiful to see the boys and girls asleep on the modernistic benches it is not yet the Sorbonne. They are not yet demanding the revolution; they are aware that this gesture is a token gesture, that Mike O'Connell will be arrested. It is the poetry of politics, and the poetry can—*halevai,* it will—lead to politics, but it is not yet politics. For Mike it is. And everyone talks about his jail sentence.

We know nothing of this and arrive for the press conference amazed at the scene around us.
Of course it must have been in the *Times,* but the news of the many sit-ins and demonstrations has become routine—like the reports of casualty figures—and unless something spectacular happens in front of a television camera, there's an inch in the *Times,* or a mildly worded column buried among the advertisements of department stores.

The students have not "occupied" this building, they are using it, and no official at M.I.T. has made any objection. Since it is nominally the "student center" and nominally belongs to the students, they think it's proper to use it as they wish. The bookshop, the cafeteria, and the various parts of the building used for extracurricular activities continue to function. So the press conference takes place as scheduled.

Julian sits on the floor of one of the classrooms and talks about theatre and revolution to a small group of journalists. The younger ones sit on the floor, the more dignified ones sit in the upholstered chairs. Isha frets and first I try to distract her by drawing on the blackboard, but after her day in the car she demands more action. I take her downstairs to the Sanctuary. Someone at the microphone is citing evidence that the bust will come between *3:00* and *4:00* A.M. Thereupon the five hundred students in the room sing eight or ten vigorous choruses of "We Shall Overcome." Ending in a rousing sentimental "We are with you, Mike, today . . ." Their fingers are raised in the V, and the few militant leftists raise their closed fists. Isha loves to hear people sing in chorus and joins in with a la-la-la.

When we return to the press conference they are discussing whether man is altruistic enough to endure the demands of a non-punitive structure.

A bearded man who is not a journalist says there cannot be a "we" and "they."
He explains that he has been living communally in the country and can't work politically until he clears up inside his head the "we" and "they." We talk about this unification. The unification of the classes that the Communists call revisionist.

We can't even unify ourselves, much less the so-called great opposing camp—"them" and "us."

The bust doesn't come that night.
Nor on Halloween. Nona hurts her back and I play the Witch of Endor in *Frankenstein* on Halloween night, waiting for the bust next door.

NOVEMBER 5, 1968:

Our son Garrick arrives. He's nineteen. We haven't seen him for more than a year. Long hair flying, his cape flying, his yellow poncho blazing, his string of beads jangling, as he runs toward us on the steps of the Kresge Auditorium. He is exuberant, everything thrills him.
We talk a lot. He had fallen into the Gene McCarthy illusion and was bitter like all who experienced that come-down. But the sight of the Sanctuary encourages him; he is

especially pleased at the organized system the students have devised, the "security," the mimeographing, the medical preparations.

I'm brought down by a late-show TV viewing of Peter Brook's *Lord of the Flies* because it seems to demonstrate the need for authority in natural man.
Sometimes I believe it.
But I can't believe for long that we are inherently evil.

Garrick plays in the *Mysteries,* reading the Brig Dollar with me both matinee and evening as he did with us in Berlin in 1965.

The Motherfuckers have come to M.I.T. and sit out on the lawn between the theatre and the Sanctuary playing with the baby.

We convince Michel, who wanted to burn his $4,000 on stage during *Paradise* in order to "destroy a part of the money-system," to give his money to the Motherfuckers instead, where it will support the weakening of the fabric better than anywhere else. He writes a check for $3,500. He will leave us now: wiser, poorer, perhaps a little enlightened, certainly sadly. He wanted to give Julian the money for The Living Theatre, but Julian refused it.

News from Germany that a Berlin friend has gotten three years for setting fire to the warehouse of the Springer newspaper empire. Jenö describes our friend's incredible brazenness in taking his action—how he went about boasting and everyone put him down as uncool. But maybe he feels like following Antigone's example:

> "I say that I did it, and I don't deny it."

Dany Cohn–Bendit was in the courtroom making such a

protest against the stiff sentence that he himself got a few days in jail.

There will be demonstrations about it, but there is little use to them, except that the continuing echo of outcries keeps sounding around the world and weakens the walls.

Garrick reads Isha *The Color Kittens,* which was his favorite book as it is hers.

Julian and I go to talk to an M.I.T. class on "Literature Today." The professor warns us that the students are reluctant to speak and makes suggestions for drawing them out. He is astonished at how they talk, how they shout and interrupt when the subject turns from "Literature Today," which bores them, to today's revolution, in which they are passionately interested.

On the eve of the election I see the last-minute last-ditch pitch of the three candidates on TV. It is telling and terrifying.

The Humphrey campaign appeals to the old-fashioned humanism: a film called *What Manner of Man,* about H.H.'s personal life—bowling and how he learned pure love from his retarded grandchild.

The Nixon campaign presents the full Madison Avenue advertising treatment: fifty gorgeous women in uniform (Air Line Hostesses for Nixon) answering white telephones linking the future president with the People. At their head pretty Julie and Tricia Nixon write down the questions; he answers coolly, statesmanlike and self-assured, saying, of course, nothing.

The Wallace film is chilling because it's the only one that's sensible. He talks about economics and international affairs. He says he will stop foreign aid which wins us enemies abroad, and build American roads that will save thousands of lives on the highways. /Autobahns?/ He warns Americans to bethink themselves of their freedom. "There are men who say to my pollsters that they will vote for me, but that they dare not admit publicly that they will vote for me because they will lose their jobs. Is that freedom?" He speaks clearly, reasonably, straight. It's a horror. The ad man's dream commercial for Nixon reeks of success.

On Election Day there is an antivote demonstration called a vote-with-your-feet-rally, one of many being held throughout the country. Julian thinks there are five hundred people. I estimate a thousand. Mostly students, with a few older new-leftists, they walk from Cambridge Green to Boston Common, where they set up their posters. A candidate from the Peace and Freedom Party makes a speech at this "Don't Vote" rally. While a patriot sings "God Bless America" under a huge placard saying "Stop the Jewish Communist Conspiracy." In the name of permissiveness both of these are tolerated. The rally is spiritless. Julian and I leave early for a rehearsal of *Paradise Now*. After we leave the police beat up the demonstrators.

The M.I.T. *Paradise* is received well by those students so stirred up in the Sanctuary. But it remains uneventful until a professor tries to stop the show and becomes the star of *Paradise*. His name, we learn, even while his tirade is going on, is Lettvin. He recently gained notoriety by taking on Timothy Leary in a hostile debate on a local radio station.

He stands up and makes his pitch in a voice fraught with urgency like those of our actors, but with a pseudo-logical approach unlike the trips of our actors. His pitch is:

"We should stop this now,
right away, because we are endangering
the Sanctuary next door."
The police, he cries, are on their way
to bust us. He insists there is pot smoking
in the theatre, and because of this
we are about to be busted. And that means
the bust will take place next door.
And Mike O'Connell will be busted.
And we should be trying to protect Mike.
And stop the playing of *Paradise*.

Steve Ben Israel—among others—reasons with him. But he's worked himself up to a paradisial pitch.

"Don't you realize you are going to be busted?"

And Steve smiles and says, "I expect it now, and every minute of my life till I die."

Of course there were no police on the way, nor was the Sanctuary busted. But the professor's performance was passionate and made a good scene, and brought the presence of the deserter into the auditorium. All night there were rumors—false, I think—that Mike O'Connell was in the theatre.

When we left the theatre the Dayglow sign SANCTUARY still shone brightly.

American hotels all come equipped with television sets and all night we watch the machines add numbers. Not until early in the morning do they decide that Nixon is to be President.
No one cares very much.
The general opinion is that one would be as bad as the other.
Yet the vote is heavy. No demonstrations disrupt the

electoral process, though many individuals made actions of dissent at certain polling places.

In *Paradise,* which takes place in the Now, the election is not even mentioned.

NOVEMBER 6, 1968:

When we arrive at Brown University to play the *Mysteries,* there are telegrams awaiting us cancelling the remaining performances at M.I.T. The reason given is that the audience cannot be controlled, that the auditorium is overcrowded and that this represents a potential fire hazard. They offer to pay us in full for the cancelled performances and also to make every effort to find us other space to perform in.
Poor *Paradise!* It has been cancelled or busted for so many different reasons:

> for making noise in the streets
> for indecent exposure
> for breach of the peace
> for too many people outside
> for too many people inside.

None of the officials will say they don't want a play that advocates anarchism.
Or perhaps they *are* saying they don't want a play that demonstrates the conditions of anarchism.

Should we protest? Should we just go away?
It is the students who should protest.
But they are properly committed to their Sanctuary scene

which is certainly more important, even as dramatic action, than our play.

There are a dozen colleges in Boston. We will look for another theatre. There is talk of free performances. Discussion and search for a theatre. Tufts, Harvard, a dozen schools make suggestions and offers, but when it comes down to it there's no way to play *Paradise* in Boston, and the ban speaks, after all, in its own voice.

NOVEMBER 8, 1968:

On the night of the cancelled *Antigone,* Garrick does patrol duty all night at the Sanctuary, and he finds it exciting standing up on the roof with the walkie-talkie, reporting the movements of the police.

But already the fervor is diminishing. There are fewer students each night, and the repeated bust scares have the "cry wolf" effect and are no longer believed and dramatic.

Julian has said all along that they would make no bust until the ardor died down. He says "they" will feed into the computer the usual duration of such enthusiasms, and come up with a date for the bust when all the strong feeling has died down.

Meanwhile, in the black ghetto of Roxbury the Martin Luther King School is closed. Even this provocation does not arouse great agitation.

Just the prerevolutionary simmering.

> People say: this is 1905, 1910, not 1917.
> This is Potemkin and St. Petersburg.

NOVEMBER 9, 1968:

On the night of the cancelled *Paradise* performance we talk with Garrick about himself and his world.
His fabulous, beloved Karen writes poetry.
He writes poetry. Melancholy poetry.
He is unabashedly nostalgic. We used to put on such airs when we were that age.

The Young: so much has despair tempered their idealism that they have become rational and magical at the same time. Contradictions don't bother them because both science and magic accept contradictions.
But their reasoning is colder, cooler and clearer than ours can ever be.
Learn wisdom from the young. And craftsmanship from the old.

And so we leave Boston with a few glimpses (three):

I. A movie: *2001*. A movie about the culture.
II. A visit to the Boston Museum of Fine Arts with Isha and Garrick. Isha walking in the Japanese shrine, Garrick zapped by my Cretan snake goddess and her shadow. Isha calls her a "doll."
III. The Sanctuary is emptied out. Swept up for a junior prom dance. The soldier, Mike O'Connell, is moved to a room upstairs, and only a few diehards are sitting with him. Did Lettvin have something to do with it? The students say so. Paranoia! He wanted us to stop playing *Paradise*, and *Paradise* has been banned.

He wanted us to make and cause no protest and we made and caused no protest.

He wanted Mike O'Connell to be protected and Mike's been moved up to the third floor, and the scenario with the walkie-talkies on the roof is over, and the posters, just beginning to flower into poetry, are taken down.

And the sensitive ones will learn that it's not enough to experience a flashing moment of enthusiasm for what is right and good, to make a revolution.
And the others, the brought-down, will find in this their proof that it's no use, and sink into despair.

NOVEMBER 10, 1968:

As we travel north from Boston to New Hampshire the climate and weather grow colder. Snow appears.

At the Brick Tower Motel in Concord, New Hampshire, Carl tells us that he heard on the radio that Mike O'Connell was busted.
There were only a few students present. There were no incidents.

NOVEMBER 12, 1968:

Driving into Vermont at the peak of the hunting season, passing car after car with a dead deer tied to its roof, or over its hood.

The towns are all decked out in American flags for the celebration of Veterans' Day.
In the snows we reach Goddard College, a retreat in the woods, with a small comfortable campus where we are housed in a homey way.
The students here are very hip. They are sheltered here in the woods.
Jules Rabin is here, he who walked with CNVA to Moscow for peace and who worked so hard with us on the General Strike for Peace.
Nina Gitana comes, bringing me a photograph of her Master, Kirpal Singh, and of her Master's Master wrapped in a peacock cloth.
She was Eurydice in *Orphée,* and she believed that she was Astarte and gave it all up to listen to the Celestial Sound at her Master's directions on an ashram in Vermont.

We play the *Mysteries* here in Goddard in a small theatre, and fully occupy the rooms given us with our enormous entourage, dozens of people who willy-nilly travel with us, children and, God help us, two monkeys. There's great dissension about who should travel in the bus.

Eight students pull our VW out of the deep snow as we leave Vermont to travel toward Pittsburgh.
On the road we stop at a Howard Johnson motel with its ridiculous fancy equipment: its infrared bathroom lights, its bedside panel for TV, radio, lights, and the weather report; its sanitized toilet, thermostat, and other specials, in Phillipsburg, N.J.
These oases of glossy plastic luxury on the bleak roads of New Jersey obliterate the last sense of traveling in a real country among real people.

NOVEMBER 15, 1968:

In Pittsburgh we perform the *Mysteries* in Skibo Hall at the Carnegie Mellon University. Leon Katz arranged the engagement. He tells us that he wants to travel with the theatre. Everyone wants to come.
It's the dream of running away with the circus.
It's the dream of running away with the Gypsies.

Before we play *Paradise* we ask to talk to the SDS students to find out where it's at. There are thirty of them in this school of thousands. They are unsure of themselves. Their aim is to get rid of the ROTC training on the campus; they make mockery of ROTC marching. They have hardly dared broach the question of the war contracts on campus, but there have been some protests against the recruitment of students by the Dow Chemical Company.
An embarrassed young man admits that he wants to get rid of ROTC because his father, who pays half his tuition, insists that *he* take ROTC. And he does.
One other SDS student is more in touch. He belongs to the War Resisters League and has attended some pacifist conferences, but he gets hardly any support here.

During the performance of *Paradise* (which is lively) the English Department approaches Leon Katz and asks in a sinister tone: "Can you defend this?"
A lady professor from Duquesne displays a letter stating that she has been forbidden to enter the campus there because she took part in a student demonstration against the use of Mace by the campus police.
Some of the students are very sent. They are the ones we play for.

NOVEMBER 18, 1968:

Back in New York. *The Queen,* Frank Simon's movie about the culture.

From New York City to Rutgers, in New Brunswick, New Jersey, where we try a new kind of lecture demonstration. Steve Ben Israel and Peter Weiss had been making experiments with breathing and body exercises for lecture demonstrations, but I found them too traditional. Now we try something new.
We begin with the Rite of Guerrilla Theatre,* but instead of ending the scene Julian explains it, talks a little about the structure of *Paradise,* and then suggests that the spectators try playing the Rite of Guerrilla Theatre. . . .
Instructions are given, the students try it, and before long the play dissolves into groups of passionate discussions à la *Paradise.*

* The Rite of Guerrilla Theatre: the first scene of *Paradise Now,* in which the performers move among the spectators and address five phrases to members of the audience:

1. I am not allowed to travel without a passport.
2. I don't know how to stop the wars.
3. You can't live if you don't have money.
4. I am not allowed to smoke marijuana.
5. I am not allowed to take my clothes off.

They repeat each phrase during two minutes, their voices and agitation rising till they scream. Then, when all have screamed, they stop and begin softly with the next phrase. At the last phrase, instead of screaming they take off their clothes to the legal limit and flash out.

NOVEMBER 19, 1968:

Then back to the snows, to Vermont. The tour takes us back and forth because plans were made at the last moment and dates conflicted and we find ourselves retracing our steps.

The company stays in a hotel in Bennington but we go up to Pawlet to Claude Fredericks' house on the hill. Lots of nostalgia. I was seventeen when Julian introduced me to Claude. He had an austere room then in a New York City brownstone, bare but for a Japanese screen of silver. The screen exists still, tarnished dark. And Claude, who teaches at Bennington, plans to go to live in Kyoto.
The house is almost unchanged. Claude's hair is long but he has not changed.
The old pine in front of the house, which Claude calls Zeus, has lost a great branch in a recent storm and it lies like a fallen warrior on the lawn where years ago we played croquet.

But all the battles are remote in the snowscape.

NOVEMBER 21, 1968:

We play *Paradise* to a vast indifferent audience at Castleton College. At a candlelit dinner in the cafeteria Mel Clay tells me Henry is busted in New York.
Paranoia.

Carl arrives next day, grim with news that it was a "real" hippie with beard and beads who busted Henry.

We play *Paradise* in the small gym at Bennington. A local commune joins us. They live in free love and they are very pretty. They take all their clothes off at the end of Guerrilla Theatre, and sit on the part of the floor marked off as the stage. And several pretty students do too—though an irate lady teacher assures me that "not one of the naked girls is a Bennington student."

Feelings run very high. The room is smaller than usual and we can take more individual trips with people.

Arthur Sainer is here, another of the General Strike for Peace people. Paranoid. He called Claude and warned him that Bennington would be burned to the ground if The Living Theatre played there, and furthermore all the students would get pregnant. But in confrontation he is pleasant and mild. I play a *Paradise* scene with him and his students:

> Do you talk about the Revolution?
> Ask my students.
> Does he teach the Revolution?
> We talk about King Lear.

NOVEMBER 22, 1968:

At a lecture demonstration at Smith College, after the Guerrilla Theatre, a discussion:

> "If you're an anarchist, why do you wear this?"
> (Pointing out my Mogen David.)
> "Well" (I start a long spiel), "if God meant us to be partners in creation . . ."
> (A pretty student, heretofore hostile, interrupts, amazed).

"You know Schlomo."
"Schlomo Carlebach? Yes."
After that there is perfect amity between us.

I have seen announcements recently of Schlomo Carlebach's concerts. Films of the Arab-Israeli war to be shown on the same program. But then his father, old Rabbi Carlebach, was proud that an American general (Julius Klein) was a member of his congregation.

> *1940:*
> But when I reproached my father with not being patriotic enough he said: "They can take my country away from me" (they had already taken Germany away from him, so why not another country?) "but they can never take my Torah away from me."

NOVEMBER 29, 1968:

Back to New York overnight and then to Philadelphia. We played The Brig here at the same YMHA in 1963, and the same ladies are selling tickets and managing things. *Antigone* and *Frankenstein* are well received. There are some snobbish people around. A lady accosts Carl in the YMHA lobby and says, "Young man, don't you think you need a bath?" and Günter reports the same insult. Neither of them answered the rude lady. But outside of these frivolous incidents all seemed to be going well in Philadelphia till the opening of *Paradise Now*.

And the performance went well. Lots of factions/ defensiveness in the Jerusalem section, Julian accused of being a "false Jew" by a man offended at our bipartisan view of the Arab-Israeli conflict, and some black women making beautiful tirades inspired by Rufus but going on into their own style: "We nursed you at our tits—we taught you—we were your slaves and at night you laid us in the bushes—" and these accusations followed by proud demands.

A good night, with a real glow at the end.

And at the end one exhilarated spectator, Ralph Harmon, runs out into the middle of Broad Street stark naked and dances around in the middle of the street and shouts:

> "I'm free.
> "I'm free."

And the cops see him.
(They have been there all along, waiting, preying.)
And he sees the cops and he runs inside for safety.
And the cops come charging in with their clubs.
And they grab Julian and Steve Ben Israel and Echnaton.

As the police approached, Julian set down the young woman he had been carrying on his shoulders. He was on the stairs, inside the building. Her young friend stepped between her and the cops. He got four stitches in his head from the clubbing and cut wrists from the handcuffs. A photographer recording this event was also busted.

> This is routine for the destruction of evidence.

I was too tired to play the last scene.

> (Much traveling has worn me down.)

I was in the dressing room. People came in, breathless.
"There's a bad scene downstairs."
I decide not to rush down. I'm sure I'd get busted. That's what I did in New Haven, and you can't really commit the same idiocy twice.

"That's my husband; can I go with him?" I had said.

And I was the only one found guilty. So I stay away.
Jenö comes in shaking.

"They're beating people up. Julian was dragged down the stairs by his hair. . . ."
"Is he hurt?"
"No, I think he's all right. Steve Ben Israel is busted.
"Peter and Karen are busted."
At this moment Karen bursts in disheveled, her hair all mussed.
"We escaped," she says.

She tells how they were on the second floor by the water cooler and a cop came up and said they were under arrest. They went with him, but as they reached the street there were a great many people and a sense of dangerous near-violence, and maybe the cop let it happen, and maybe the crowd scared him, and maybe it's because they are dancers.
In the lobby, witnesses, dozens of them, are writing down what they saw. Mel Clay is organizing this activity with a lawyer from the Y named Goldstein. Bob Cohen has called Projansky, who is still busy with Henry's case.
A beautiful peace creature named Ira Einhorn has called the best lawyer in town, who handles all the peace people's trials.

At the station house, Bob handles reporters. No one knows what the charges are. V signals. A Japanese journalist crosses beyond the sergeant's desk. They pounce on him,

throw him inside. Reporters. They throw him back out. "I was only looking for the men's room." "Get out of here, boy."
To the newly built jail described as an eight-shape, or an infinity sign, but Shari says correctly: in the shape of handcuffs.
We wait till 9:00 A.M. while night court grinds out its heartless scenes.
The same smart-aleck judge I've seen for years, laughing at prostitutes, mocking the unfortunate.
A large good-humored court officer plays clown and straight man to the judge. The prisoners come in handcuffed.
A club has been busted and the court officer makes leering remarks about the women, who are nervous and brazening it out. Some drunken drivers, some assault cases, one youngster getting a minor charge dismissed because he is up for murder.

At six the judge and the court recorder leave, and everybody else waiting around sleeps all over the floors and the modernistic benches.
There's a hot-dog stand outside, open all night, as is the brightly lit bail bondsman office:

> Beyond the bondsman's gaudy sign can be seen the exquisite architecture, exquisitely lit, of Independence Hall, the birthplace of our freedom.

Charles Butterworth is here. All the old names from the General Strike reappear. It was he who was busted at the Catholic Worker while protecting an escaped convict who was washing the dishes in the house of hospitality. He is straight, serious and unsmiling.

I talk all night with Ira Einhorn, who tries to make out a case for astrology as a "matrix." He's both smart and good.

The new judge doesn't arrive until nine. The lawyer talks with him on friendly terms. Then they bring out our criminals in handcuffs.

If the judge is more respectful to us than to the poor, it's only because we have those three smart lawyers. If the judge is more respectful to us than to the poor,

it's rotten, rotten, rotten all the way down the line.

A date is set for three days hence (Friday) and nominal bail of one dollar each.

/The standard bail for the poor—who can't raise it—
$300. "Them that has gets."
Ingrate. I should be grateful for privilege: would I
not complain more bitterly if the bail had been high?
Yes, I would indeed. I'll complain either way./

The three who were inside witnessed a different scene from what we saw in the polite courtroom. The prisoners were greeted by the police with howls of derision, and mockingly called "the Israelities." There were roars of laughter and a mock chorus of "Here comes Moses, let mah people go, hey, Pharaoh, here come the Israelites." And so on for six hours of unrelenting tirade. I asked how they maintained their cool and managed not to talk back, and Steve Ben Israel says the cops were so anxious to provoke a cause for using their hands that it wasn't hard to try to avoid giving them an "excuse." Not that they need one, but there's a certain cool that can protect you up to a point.

The same fat officer that spoke so humbly and formally to his "honor" went back to the prison part and talked like a racist to those whom he brought out in handcuffs.
Julian says he has never seen police quite so brutalized and

crass. Not in terms of brutality or violence but in terms of ugly behavior toward prisoners—a kind of scornful hatred. He says their faces bore a snarling look that made the current insulting appellation of "pig" seem fitting. I was amazed that he would say that, he who pleads for compassion for the police.

But that was while driving home in someone's jeep, through the Philadelphia morning crowd and the Christmas shoppers, after submitting silently to six hours of anti-Semitism, and the suffering still fresh.

Carl says that it is not worse in Philadelphia, it is worse in November 1968. He points out that as the state system rigidifies, the police are trained more and more to "separate themselves from the people, and so they are encouraged to treat prisoners in a different way," as they begin to regard themselves less and less as "civilians."

Though I've been clubbed and kicked and cursed at during arrests I've always been treated politely in every jail I've been in, and always managed a cool relationship with the jailers and the jail cops.

A brief exception in Paris, when I was manhandled and thrown into a cell on my ass, was resolved when, with a little work on the language barrier, we were able to talk to the policeman and got across to him more or less. And we talked and smiled. I've never faced a really hostile or vicious guard in a jail, and it scares me to imagine being at the mercy of someone hostile—in fact it is remarkably hard for me to imagine this.

We talk of the Munich arrests, when Rufus and Shari were held with loaded guns at their heads.

I think I would pass out if someone pointed a loaded gun at me.

What kind of talk is that?
I don't know. Maybe . . . if it really came to it, I like to think I'd be brave. So far when I've been hit by police I've always been cool and taken the moment very matter of factly. . . .

Times Square, Stockholm, Rue de la Huchette

. . . and I've never been frightened, but then I've always been convinced at that moment that no real harm was intended.
There's some ambiguity here.
Trust and Caution are in conflict.

After the "white night" and the strain of the courtroom scene, I'm too sick and weak (with a cough) to perform the lecture-demonstration at Temple University.
Racked by coughing, I wait in the car, and wander a little around the decrepit black ghetto that surrounds this large Philadelphia university.
Julian's energy is unflagging and incredible.
After the *Paradise* rehearsal, after the night in jail, he conducts the lecture-demonstration and then drives to New York.

The lawyers talk of saving a trip to Philadelphia by pleading guilty, but it seems immoral in view of what happened, and all the witnesses, and seeing that the Y is bringing suit against the police for their uninvited entrance into the building.
So Julian and Echnaton and Steve Ben Israel go to Philadelphia and play the courtroom scene—and Julian does a thing with the judge—and the judge asks him many metaphysical questions. And acquits them on all but one of the smaller technical charges. Obstructing an officer, or breach of peace, or one of those no-crime crimes which exist

to justify the police—so that it doesn't look as though the cops bust people, especially artists and names-in-the-paper-image people, for nothing.
And so the small fine is paid.
And the effects and causes of law and order are once again made painfully clear to a small group of onlookers. That's not a technique, it's an unfortunate side effect. But like history, inevitable.

NOVEMBER 30, 1968:

At Princeton a stuffy audience like a German Stadthalle subscription audience looks at the *Mysteries* with a cold fishy eye.
The Princeton Theatre advertised it so vulgarly that hardly any students come, only bored bourgeois theatregoers looking for a prurient thrill and finding none of that in the *Mysteries* in spite of the posters asking "Put On or Turn On?" Yet, as always, a few nice students.

It's for them.

DECEMBER 1, 1968:

Back in New York there are conferences with Jim Spicer about a book including Julian's and my diaries, letters pertaining to theatre, etc; with Wynn Chamberlain about a screen treatment of *Paradise*. Rubin Gorewitz comes to go over the accounts. He brings a bug detector, the dials of which indicate that the telephone at 800 West End Avenue is not tapped, but that there is a bugging device somewhere outside the window.

In Great Neck we play *Antigone* in a synagogue. The audience is enthusiastic. They are mostly middle-class (rich) Jewish intellectuals, local culture vultures. In the third row are Julian's brother and that branch of the family; and as always some beautiful students.

Henry Howard out on bail. Very serious, and when he's serious he's beautiful, and all that cocky bullshit goes, and he gets thoughtful and intelligent.
He had a hard time in jail, and he too reports that the cops are bad.
He said one guard was playing his Brig role of Grace with all its crass sadistic humor, and he thought, "You're good, we could have used you." But there are horror stories too. And his mood, like the mood of everyone just out of jail, is fear. Everyone chips in his salary for the bail and he makes a thank-you speech to which he attaches a warning about the dangers of living free in the world.

Steve Ben Israel brings a copy of Abbie's book, *Revolution for the Hell of It.*
Abbie's hospitalized with hepatitis.
Allen Ginsberg's hospitalized by a car accident along with the Orlovskys.
I joke: "Who's the third?" Julian mocks: "Don't be superstitious."
Accidents in threes. They die in threes.
Please don't be superstitious.
Abbie's book is beautiful. He says: "Don't argue with brothers."

It has no author; the first person of the narrative calls himself "Free"—"and then Free said,"—and the book is credited on the title page to "Free."
On the cover is a picture of Abbie by Richard Avedon, the word FREE printed clearly on his forehead.

> (I said: "They are going to bust you, Abbie," but he said, "For what? I didn't do anything. They can't bust me for writing the word 'Fuck' on my forehead." He did that at the HUAC hearings.)

On the back cover is an Avedon photo, not posed, of Abbie being busted by two cops.

The tensions mount. So imperceptibly, they are the hour hands.
The daily demonstrations, busts, protests, vocabulary changes are the minute hands.
Inside the twisting heads, visible only to the inner eye—the second hands.

DECEMBER 2, 1968:

We drive to Scranton. Grim town, grim scenery. The Hong Kong flu hits nine members of the company.
Everybody's nervous and tense and down. Luke and Pierre Devis talk of leaving the company and waiting for us in Europe.
Rufus, Petra, Birgit, Cal, Pierre laid low with flu.
Tai and Ali and Chiwe—flu.

The "Walker Report," a commissioned report on the Chicago riot, comes out with scandalous repercussions. It

calls the Chicago scene a "police riot." The media make a great to-do about it.
My own reaction is that such a report will have, alas, a more effective backlash of anger and repression than positive results. But I'm a pessimist. Of course it's good that it's said that the police were violent and brutal, but a fink report is not a revolutionary document.

In the Scranton University gym, a performance of *Mysteries.* A cop pushes a young woman on a stairway—only to clear the aisle, but not very politely. A hundred voices begin to cry out, "Pig," and it's very frightening. The cop cools it (there are four cops, four thousand students). Jimmy Tiroff, maybe a little drunk, goes up to the cop, puts a fraternal arm around him, and in a snarling, theatrical American voice says loudly "Ah don't pay no mind to them, they're just the audience and we, we're cops." Everything was cooled by the madness of this remark. Well and good, but there was something wrong in the way the accusative term was thrown at the men.
Something wrong in calling out a word or a sound that has no meaning but hate.
It does not enlighten or instruct or help.
The same is true of crying out "Fascist" or "Nazi."
Slowly and insidiously a mantel of hatred covers over the revolution of love; there is cause to cry out.

When we think of the poor and the victims it is not hard—

> (the blacks, the sharecropper, the factory slaves, the napalmed)

—it is not hard to comprehend their hatred, and say, "Of course they hate."
And they need the alliance of the students, the young

intellectuals, the sons of the bourgeoisie bent on betraying their exploitative natal class by siding with the victims. Is it necessary that they join the victims in their outcries of rage and hatred?

They say it is. And I say rage, yes, and hatred, no. I find myself in an unpopular corner. I'm getting wedged in. Can't call a man "pig" because it makes it too easy to suggest the slaughter. Am an outnumbered vegetarian, and the animal slayers are all around, and the gruesome slogan is changed already:

"Kill the Pig, spill his blood."

DECEMBER 5, 1968:

We travel from Scranton to Granville, Ohio, across the cool country.

Grim landscapes, smog, pathetic drab mining towns, slag hills, huge industrial plants with nightmare scenery, or small decrepit mines and enterprises with depressing gray structures. The highway cuts through a dreary part of Wheeling, West Virginia. Makes one think, "How can people live that way?" and opens the vista of the whole world working at hateful work, at hated labor, begrudging the hours and years, longing for something unknown, better, but something conceivable only in terms of "being rich."

And on the road through this pathos the only available lodgings are the fancy motels that offer us their plastic sumptuousness, with paper bands around the toilet seats that say "sterilized," and on their television:

A) Student riots: San Francisco, New York City. Images of students and police battles.

B) A phone-in program on which two SDS students from Marquette, who had participated in a demonstration against the carrying of Mace by the campus police, patiently bore an hour of insults (you Communists should have your heads kicked in, etc.) and tried to defend their idealistic views against a collection of nasty, snarling, threatening callers. The discouraging sound of the American voice.

C) A Supreme Court justice defends the law as though it were noble and beautiful and didn't hire armed men to beat, jail, and kill those who disagree with it and won't submit.

Around us the lands of the Indian Mounds.

DECEMBER 7, 1968:

Toward Cincinnati. Everyone has the Hong Kong flu. The news full of unrest: a school in Harlem closed. Six hundred cops with drawn guns in San Francisco. Three Black Panthers busted in New Jersey. Twenty Russian intellectuals in a street demonstration in Red Square: no arrests. A strike at the Renault factory in Paris. All of Italy out on strike to protest the killing of striking workers by police in Sicily.

In Cincinnati we play in the Playhouse in the Park, where a rather stodgy audience attends this subscription theatre, built on top of a hill overlooking the city, to which no means of transportation is available except private car or taxi. A theatre for the rich. We do *Mysteries, Frankenstein, Antigone*. No *Paradise*. And they applauded, not much, rather bored by us, except, of course, for a few students, and it's for them.

Everyone has the flu. Between a *Mysteries* matinee and an evening *Antigone* we rehearse replacements, all of us in various stages of discomfort, fevers, coughing, chills.

DECEMBER 9, 1968:

We drive from Cincinnati, Ohio, to Ann Arbor, Michigan. The grim towns give way to rich farmlands, broad fields with huge farms. I wish I could read the landscape. All through Europe it disturbed me that I could look and see so little. But there I could excuse myself, lamely, as an alien. I feel it more and more acutely.
What grows in these fields? Who are these people?
How do they live? What do they do?
They eat hamburgers and fried potatoes. I see them every day. But their landscapes tell me so little. I recognize the poor, and the rich, but I can barely distinguish barren ground from fruitful ground.
I can tell their voices in the luncheonettes: some places the tone is gentler than others, but the poor everywhere imply intimacy by bantering insults.
I can tell their voices, hostile or tender, but the color of the soil tells me little.
It would be good to go across this landscape with a guide who would tell the story of these cows and those cows.

In Ann Arbor there is a little hotbed. The revolutionary students are full of life and they seem not to have felt the big down that the season has brought.

"Underground films" in a regular movie house starting at 11:00 P.M. W. C. Fields. The Chicago Scene.

> The Change of Seasons.
> The Official Yippie (Youth International Party) statement on Chicago.

A serious and gay view using a lot of the same material. The movie house jammed with hip youngsters. Lots of cheers when the newsreel face of the spokesman for the Chicago police says, "These people aren't just demonstrating, these people want to destroy the government."

Ann Arbor harbors the seeds of the White Panther Movement and its fierce-maned spokesman John Sinclair.*

When we meet he embraces me and calls me sister, in that Muslim way which I find friendly.

The word comrade is hard for the American ear. Even the young have trouble with its echo of the hard Old Left and its ill fame in the old anti-commie jokes and hokey movies. But the word brother, as the blacks use it, has a warm, religious quality, almost mystical, but familial in its implication of the deepest of ties.

The White Panther policy statement was printed in the Detroit *Free Press,* one of the good underground papers. They support the Black Panther movement including its violent aspects; though violence is not their special thing they condone the use of it; they are bold and wild, their policies are anarchist and expressed in the hot jargon of the streets (e.g., "free dope and fucking in the streets"). They

* In 1969 John Sinclair was sentenced to ten years for giving away two joints of marijuana to a federal agent. Free John Sinclair!

are beautiful and somehow they are my brothers. My violent brothers.
My brother Cain with the marked forehead.
It is with shuddering that I accept their pin, the white panther prowling forward on a purple background.
But I can't wear it.
I am afraid. I am afraid it is too late for peace.

To make a tape of *Paradise* that can be copyrighted for Wynn to make a movie version, Julian and I seek out a room with a little privacy and Jimmy Anderson's tape recorder. We work in a student house called Nakamura. The new style of community. The students live in messy informality. The individual rooms differ in style, many quite scholarly and many in total disorder. Next to a room of neat books is a room covered floor to ceiling with graffiti; some rooms house one student and some more hospitably house four or five and several additional guests from The Living Theatre. There's an ambiance of the Catholic Worker. All the posters and writing call for permissiveness.

In Ann Arbor—an air of Nanterre.

Julian gives a lecture for the Michigan State College students.

Thomas Merton dies in Bangkok, electrocuted by the faulty wiring of an electric fan.

Isha is feverish. Everyone still plagued by the flu. No time to work.

DECEMBER 11, 1968:

The students have hired a room for us to play in in the students' building, called Union Hall; in the lobby there is an aggressive air.
Upstairs an air of carnival.
Permissiveness. Balloons. Freedom. Hand clapping.
Abbie Hoffman says: The Movement = Dancing.

I look for a serious face: Paul Melton's appears.
We knew him at the Catholic Worker. Now he runs the antiwar coffee shop in the town, where the students and soldiers gather.
After *Paradise* we meet with him. He feeds the whole company, free, and then we make our way to his cellar room and speak of all the problems.

He was on his way to Israel when we saw him last. It was during the time when we were calling for the General Strike for Peace. Paul asked me if there were any messages or questions for Buber, whom he intended to visit.
I asked him to ask about the enormous despair.
Now, years later and the old man dead, Paul brings the return message.
He describes the house where Buber lived:
"He was under a kind of tacit house arrest. The house was part shrine and part prison. They revered and honored him and at the same time abhorred his attempt to make peace with the Arabs."
And he went on to tell us about their talk and about the discussion of the General Strike for Peace, and then he asked if there was any message or advice for us and he said Buber rose and embraced him and said, "Give them this."
And he rose and he hugged Julian

and he hugged me
with a hug from the old dead teacher.
The icy winds of Lake Michigan blew a soft spray of snow across the streets of Ann Arbor above the ceiling of the cold cellar where we sat—
To the desert sands blowing around the windows of Buber's house, to the warm intention of the old man's hug.

Then we talked about the present and about farming, and about the formation of communities.
"For nine years I've been trying to grow soy, and I've had nine failures."
As to the plans of some of the members of The Living Theatre to do some farming, he says they must have "the cooperation of someone who knows the ground"; and if it's an American he suggests "someone who has been farming for several generations, though any twelve-year-old Japanese would know how to make the soil yield."

Then we talked about the blacks and the violence.

Then we talked about Thomas Merton's death. Bangkok? A badly wired electric fan? "CIA," says Paul.
Paranoia.

Then we talked about the resistance movement, and the deserters and the real underground.
He is going to make a theatre of the cellar. He asks us about a director.
When we leave he tries to fill our arms with bread and jars of preserves.
There's peace in this Ann Arbor hotbed, as well as violent revolutionary fervor.

DECEMBER 14, 1968:

In Detroit we play at the respectable Detroit Institute of Art. Sam Wagstaff, one of the art directors, had befriended us (once somewhere in some European city) and we talk about "long hair" with him as if it were some major political issue. For a whole dinner we talk about nothing but long hair, and he is really "into" this "problem" because he "understands about it" and is shocked that others do not. He is impeccably groomed (neat short hair), and highly civilized.

At the museum, the best things are the Rivera Murals, which are a crazy put-on, put-down, of the entire Ford Motor scene; eloquent and sad and poetic, surrounded by Renaissance art ("A fine collection!") on one side and a temporary exhibit of "Modern French Art" on the other.

Fredy Perlman, last seen among the Yugoslavian Albanians, is now in Detroit. He helps set up platforms for the stage as though he had been with us all along. I ask him about the Albanians.
"This is the time to be here," he says enthusiastically. He is editing a violent anarchist magazine, *Red and Black*. Full of outspoken rage and stirring up much feeling.
I read it during the *Antigone* rehearsal and its despair of any alternatives but violence makes me very sad.

He was in Paris in May, he says, and narrowly missed us in several places, including the Odéon. We exchange remembrances of the exhilaration of those days and the spirit of the French students.
And I say that for all that, they were not violent. In spite of the "*pavés*"—or am I deluding myself as to the extent and intent of those incidents?

I am torn, but not in half.
Ultimately my source is in the moment when I knew: "I must have no hatred or bitterness toward anyone." And if that is now not to be a revolutionary principle then to that extent (and to that extent only, by the rotten semantics of it) I am not a revolutionary. And that thought may make me crazy. But not crazy enough to kill my fellow.
I said it of the Nazis and I'll say it of the cops: If you hate and if you kill, it's always the same trap.
And I was considered crazy by my family then when I couldn't hate the Nazis enough (I hated them, but not enough), and I'm considered "reactionary" now by certain comrades because I won't hate the cops enough,
and I'm badly torn but not in half.
I know on which side life is.

At a "party" at a sculptor's cooperative some ministers of the White Panther Party talk big about cop scenes. They do this to put me on because I speak of peace. They carry on about "the pig" and how they outwitted him, or how he beat on them, or how they beat up on him, as if they were schoolchildren using dirty words in front of a prudish teacher.
And they succeeded, not in shocking me, but in further making me very sad.
They channelled the substance of their revolutionary fervor into "getting the pig" and there was no hopefulness in them.
One of them was a painter and we were surrounded by his despairing paintings of blood-spattered women hanging dripping male genitalia on hooks. And deformed people and Thalidomide children.

DECEMBER 15, 1968:

En route from Detroit to Ithaca we foolishly decide to stop and see Niagara Falls. Pierre Biner is riding in our car and we can't go to the Canadian side because he has no re-entry permit. We were suddenly on a long bridge, having passed a toll booth where a friendly toll man wished us a pleasant morning, and remarked on the briskness of the weather.
Suddenly the flags turn Canadian in mid-bridge.
We come to another toll house at the end of the bridge.
Its sign says: "Welcome to Canada."
"We don't want to go to Canada," says Julian.
"Oh, all right, if you don't want to go to Canada," says the uniformed man, "I'll back you up," and he directs our car back around the bridge.
When we come to the American side we are asked for identification. We said we weren't in Canada, and asked him to check with the man at the other end of the bridge or the man here, a few booths away, who had greeted us and talked about the weather. They said they could do neither, questioned us, asked for passports. Checked us out in their books of unwanted characters and harassed Pierre about his re-entry permit. And I was angry because Isha was sleeping and I wanted to keep going, and they let me go back out to the baby after they checked my passport in their books.

Then I see a cop arrive, pull up beside our car, and go inside the building.
The cop enters the building with his gun drawn. Julian tells me what happened. The customs man says to the cop, "It's all right. I got a G15 here, but I thought it was something

worse." The cop relaxes. Finally they check with the Canadian side and it's cool.
Then, when it was over, they asked Julian to sit down. Asked him about his travels, about his passport stamps, about travel to Iron Curtain countries, and finally "Have you been to Cuba?"
After a while Julian asks, "What's a G15?" It's not his business, it's a designation they use.
As we drive away from this aggressive border we see the cops carefully searching Renfrew's and Gianfranco's car.

That's how the American paranoia is made. Out of nothing. An atmosphere of distrust is created, a fiction, full of sinister numbers.

> "I got a G15 . . . but I thought it was something worse."

We stop at the Horseshoe Falls on the American side. Air full of spume, icy and very windy. A gray light over the noisy water.

DECEMBER 18, 1968:

We drive to Ithaca, where we live in a motel and play at Cornell. Then drive to Rochester and play *Paradise* and drive back till 6:00 A.M., and then play *Paradise* at Cornell.

I have the flu and Isha has the flu.
In Rochester we visit the cops before the show to cool them out.

"Top cops" are always polite.

In Ithaca we hear that our contract to play *Paradise* and *Antigone* again in Boston has been cancelled because of the terrible things written about us in the *Boston Globe* in a Sunday magazine article. Hancock Hall had apparently had its license revoked because of our coming, or as I later heard, had "asked" to have its license temporarily revoked so as not to have us play there.
Word comes from New York (from Saul) that Ted Mann, who has the Henry Miller Theatre on Broadway, will let us have a guarantee of four midnight performances there. We have objected to all attempts to get us to play Broadway

(the heart of cultural darkness).

But now, under the financial duress of the loss of the Boston gig, we talk about playing there reluctantly, and with an apology about how our possibilities were narrowing down: Banned in Avignon, Geneva, Boston, busted in New Haven and Philadelphia. But we are saved from this fate by some students in Boston who hire a hall for us to play in Roxbury.

DECEMBER 22, 1968:

Roxbury. Boston's Harlem. And as hot. The hall, The Crown Manor, is a catering hall, decorated for bar mitzvah and wedding receptions. The hall is also used for community meetings by the new black management.

The vice squad comes to inquire. There is a rumor that we

may be arrested. The lawyers are there and so are the police. The management tells the cops they can come in as his guests, but they had better behave like gentlemen.

The cops are very conspicuous in the midst of the hip students.

We don't know yet how to focus the audience's energy. But the cops are easier to deal with. Their reluctance is simpler. It's easier to rouse them out of their slumber than to clarify the confused ideology of the violent revolutionary. But not as important to us. For they (the cops) will forget that they dug us for a moment and revert to the violence of their rule book. But the radical students . . . well?

When we went to the huge police headquarters in Rochester we talked across the polished table like diplomats.

> "Be assured that we are not anxious for any difficulties."
> "Nor, of course, are we."

But in *Paradise* we can talk to them as men, and we are present with them.
After the play Steve Ben Israel asked some of them about the obscenity and they said they didn't find it obscene and he asked them to wonder why they were sent to harass us and who sent them.
The paranoia's terrible.
Always thinking about the police. And when a young man undressed at the end of the Guerrilla Theatre, lawyer Bob Projansky walked to him and said "I'm the lawyer. There are fifteen cops on either side of you."
The young man dressed.
Growing paranoia.

DECEMBER 23, 1968:

We travel to New York.

The Apollo moonship is launched on television.

Carol Berger weeps. She is very sick and faces surgery. Fear.

DECEMBER 24, 1968:

In New York, there is Garrick, full of enthusiasm.
His friends gather, joyous, high, filled with the sense of being involved in something good, important and interesting.
They are not angry, not enraged.
They are disdainful in a pleasant way of old-left tactics, but they are clearly political. Their culture is their revolution. They are not hung up by their "problems" but allow that there are problems. They look openly at the problems, hopeful of finding ways to work them out. No despair, no divided loyalties. It gives one hope.

DECEMBER 27, 1968:

A visit with Salvador Dali. He sits in the bar at the St. Regis Hotel surrounded by fancy women and interesting young men. He chats with each one in turn, in French and English. The women talk about their careers, each one—

actress, model, rock-and-roll singer, big blonde—working very hard. The men are quieter, and Dali makes general remarks about their appearance, praising them to the ladies.

Of Tony Kinna: He is a Raphael! Look, a Raphael!
Of Garrick: Gothic. Very Gothic!
Of Sandy: *Très beau, très, très beau!*

To Julian, Dali speaks more seriously, in French, of a new book about himself by Pauwels, and of the excellent reception of The Living Theatre in Spain.
Julian describes the Spanish censorship of *Antigone*.
Dali says that it will soon be better in Spain, because within the year there is to be the restoration of the monarchy. He has spoken lately to Juan Carlos and it is all ready to happen and then there will be a great age in Spain. When more young people arrive, filling up the adjoining table, Dali bids no one change places, he, himself, will change places. He raises his gold cane, and in his magnificent velvet suit and lace accessories he climbs up over the chairs and benches and sits at the adjoining table. As he is now next to Garrick and me, I question him about the restoration of the monarchy.

/Not aggressively, of course; I only ask if it is a theory or a practical possibility./

He assures me that of course it is an actuality. Franco is old, he says, and the Royalists are energetic. Then he describes his utopian vision.

"It is the ideal situation. A king on top, a sensitive, artistic, intelligent monarch.
"No bourgeoisie. Only a king, and an aristocracy. And underneath, the anarchists, who want to kill the king. What a wonderful tension, what a life spirit."
He gestures. Above, the king. Below, the anarchists.

His scenario is clear and romantic.
I imagine that he sees himself in the brilliant court, painting the royal splendor, eating at the royal table.
But secretly, in the dungeons, plotting with the beautiful young anarchists with the fervent faces and naked torsos, protecting them, helping them secretly, saving them from the gallows, delivering secret messages, planning escapes, and painting them too, painting the sufferings of the people, painting the incongruity of life on earth.

G
"Dali contre la culture Bujoise pour la nouvelle Aristocracie
l *1968"*
a

reads the inscription in the book Dali sends us through Rufus.
With Garrick we leaf through the pages dwelling on the magical and mathematical effects.
It's all there, in all the religious and secular works.
Bread and Glory.
Anarchists and aristocrats.
The fantasy and the pre-utopian actuality.

JANUARY 1, 1969:

On New Year's Day Dali arranges a dinner "for a few European friends" and "le Living." The setting is classic. At the desk of the St. Regis we are directed to the wine cellar. It is no restaurant; it is the real wine cellar, though on the ceiling of the bottle-lined room plastic grapes are hung.

The table is decorated as if for Christmas. The room is very crowded, quite dark, and everything in it sparkles.

There are three Spanish noblemen.

Gala presides up center in a dress of lavish lamé. At her left, the youngest of the Spanish noblemen, who sits, not facing the table but facing Gala, and never looks away from her. Dali seats me to his right, and to the left of Gala's young man. Taking a hint from this young man I sit with one elbow on the table, facing Dali, who sits back from the table, to greet and seat and to rearrange newcomers. He comments on the beautiful disorder. Julian is sitting next to Ultraviolet. Garrick, raising his eyes to heaven—or the plastic grapes—sits between one of the charming Spaniards and a black singer in a very fancy dress.

Dali talks to me for a quarter of an hour.

He speaks of the new era in Spain.

He says a great deal that I do not fully understand because he is speaking rapidly in French.

He speaks of getting The Living Theatre a castle in Spain or a deserted village in the district from which he comes.

He speaks of all the people at the dinner party, commenting on each in turn around the table. Of Garrick he says:

> "He looks like a Vermeer."
> I: "Last time you said he looked Gothic."
> Dali: "That was in a different light."
>
> He speaks of art.
> He speaks of the aristocratic position of the artist.

There is only a tossed salad for vegetarians (plus five wines —first French, then Spanish—and coffee and cake), so it is not hard to remain facing him, eating only when he rises to greet a newcomer or say farewell to someone leaving. He seems to appreciate this.

I sit and stare at him like a stupid woman, still only half understanding him. Sometimes nodding approval or sharing his disdain or his profundities. And like a stupid woman I succeed so that when I am finally driven to express my inadequacy he pooh-poohs me:

"It is not the words, you understand me completely."

His face is handsome. He is easy to watch.

When Serge Obolensky comes in, Dali seats the old prince next to me and goes off to talk to Julian. Obolensky has a British accent. His English is splendid.
No American or Russian intonations. He looks like a British nobleman from Central Casting.
He speaks with feeling, like an actor playing a very touching, very heroic character.

He is the Heart of Darkness!

He pours out his life story, several times considerately inquiring whether I find it boring. It was not. Though I shuddered several times.

The aristocracy, he tells me, is based on courage and ability. And to illustrate this theory he tells me the history of his family, how they came from the north, his illustrious ancestors, and conquered Europe. Knowing little of this sequence of history I sense the greatness of his ancestors only by the fierce look with which the old man speaks of them.

The hardness, the iciness on which he prides himself!
That British stiffness, that high-class coldness, rigidity.
Frozen world.
Thaw! Thaw!

Tells me of the Romanoffs, his cousins, and the poor Czarina, "who had to sleep with her door open to hear

her child in the next room: hemophilia, mustn't hurt himself,
you know, very tragic, unfortunate woman.

"But then afterwards when I was hiding from the
Bolsheviks I lived hidden in the house of an actress of the
Moscow Art Theatre. You see, I know the life of actors,
I hid there a long time. Very interesting woman . . .

"Then afterwards I came to America and I liked it here
and went into business life with my brother-in-law, Vincent
Astor. And I became a paratrooper and then even the
Bolsheviks respected me. After the battle of Stalingrad,
we officers, Americans and Bolsheviks, toasted each other
(I was a colonel) and the Bolshevik general asked me if I
wanted to come back. I said I preferred America.
Do I bore you with these stories? It is interesting, isn't it?"

"And now I am devoting myself to the most important
work of my career. I am devoting myself to the President's
Crime Commission. We must stop the anarchy in the
streets—and these student disorders—
I have seen the Bolshevik Revolution—I know what it is.
We must be strong, we must apply the whip. I'm right,
am I not?"

"Ah, I am a pacifist, and therefore I must say you are too
hard. You are wrong."

He smiles. He takes my hand, which is resting on the
table, and covers it with his hand.
"You speak as a woman."

"Yes, as a woman and not as a politician.
"And as a Jew—"

(JEW!?!)

"Yes, as a Jew I point out that the Temple has two pillars

and we are bidden always to temper justice with mercy."
He presses his hand over mine on the red tablecloth. I
hardly breathe.
I weigh the wisdom of shouting:

Up against the wall, Motherfucker! as he says

"That's all right, for a *woman* to be a pacifist, but we,
we men, must be strong and firm, and stamp out the anarchy
in the streets. The students must be whiplashed."

He sees me change faces.
"I understand," he says (of course he understands nothing
but the treachery of the ruling class to their fellow-men),
"but I must be firm, I must, I cannot for your sake,"

/for *my* sake! I almost am moved to kick over the
whole fancy table, wines, crystals, princes, candles,
and dead turkeys, but I hold on. There must be a
better way, a wiser one./

"I cannot for your sake—*not* apply the whip."
I draw my hand away from under his.
"Yes for my sake . . . softer . . . less hard."
And I find my hand coming down pretty hard (a vehement
clasp, between rage and pleading, but still inside the
convention.)
"Less hard, you are too hard, too hard—" and just then
Dali interrupts, and Julian, to say we must leave for the
play. And we leave the wine cellar reeking with madness.
The prince and the court painter find us charming.
And we will find a way to topple their bloodsucking
dreams of empire.

It is good that I was silent.
When I cry out, I don't want to make a scene.
When I cry out I want the walls to come tumbling down.

Later we learn that we have a friend who knows Obolensky. Our friend says that his wife is the long-time object of Obolensky's passion (that hot hand again). Our friend says he will ask his wife to try to dissuade him from doing this dirty work, but I say, let her see him and let him do the dirty work (for they can always find another princeling for their whiplashing), and let's learn through him and her what the Crime Commission is up to, what they know, what they don't know, what they fear, what they don't fear, who's working for them, their methods—these things are valuable to the revolutionaries. "Aha," says our friend, "my wife's always wanted to be a double agent."

That's all fantasy. Sometime I think the whole American scene is just a bad flash of a nightmare.
The most paranoid people seem realistic.

John Harriman appears (from Morocco) at a meeting at Wynn Chamberlain's to discuss the *Paradise Now* film. Jenny is in Africa because Spain was too cold.

JANUARY 2, 1969:

Paradise performances are getting too prolonged and talky. There are two actions: tirade and group rap. Group rapping is quiet and generally intellectual. Tirades are vehement, dramatic, scary and emotional.
The audience participation is too predictable in its forms and too limited: stamping and handclapping, and swaying that derives from the Chord and our other rituals.
No politics.

Actors move among the audience and engage individuals or groups in intense discussions.
While Julian, Steve Ben Israel, Rufus Collins, Mel Clay, and Echnaton and Luke engage in outbursts of vehement tirade.
Garrick attends the Bronx *Paradise* and gets very involved and takes all his clothes off and talks eloquently.

On the second of January we move from the Poe Forum in the Bronx

> The old Loew's 167th Street, a huge, dusty hole, the dirt of years and disuse obscuring the movie palace splendors of other days.
> "See that chandelier?" asks an old stagehand. "That once cost $18,000." He surely exaggerates, but the point is made. "And yesterday I cranked it down and up again and it filled the whole place with dust." Now it is covered in a metal mesh net and looks like a great burst of lighted dust, not a crystal showing. The whole place is a nightmare of filth. The young people come here and like the atmosphere—but they are not political. Enthusiastic, vibrant, but not political. The dust is only stirred.

to the smooth clean auditorium of Hunter College. On the site of the old elementary school where I learned to count and to read.
In its modern transmutation built after the great fire.

> *1935:*
> One day when I was nine I came to school and the building on Park Avenue and sixty-eighth Street was a smoldering wreckage, smoke still rising from its fire-

> gutted hulk. A Hunter College student called my mother—"Hello, Mrs. Malina? Judith's school just burned down . . . but she's all right"—and sent me back home. After that we went to school in the Sunday school rooms of Temple Emmanuel while they built this great modern box in which we play now.

During *Antigone* a young man with far-out eyes gets on the stage and asks us to stop the performance because the Messiah has come. He insists that we must believe him. He says, "You'll read it in the *Times* tomorrow morning." The audience appeals to him to leave. He finally does, but only after a long disruption of the scenes with his Messianic message.

The Hunter audience is middle class. They watch. No hope.

We talk to the young man later in the dressing room. He wants to partake of Instant Redemption but wavers between transcendence and despair.

And that's where it's at for many of them.

The goal is vague, the way muddled and dark.

JANUARY 6, 1969:

We go to a meeting at one of the communal lofts on the East Side, where plans are being made for demonstrations in Washington on Inauguration Day. Mobilization for Peace has planned a careful program ranging from workshops and discussion groups to a play called *The Inaugura-*

tion of Pegasus P. Pigg according to Sirhan Sirhan. And they have a permit for a tent set up on the site of the Poor People's Resurrection City.

> Resurrection City that met the fate of the poor—
> outwitted, outnumbered, and done out of everything,
> leaving their muddy huts, busted at that, and down
> in the dumps without their great leader. Wasn't that a
> strategy: to take a roots movement and build up its
> head to unmanageable proportions, to build up its head
> man by giving him a Nobel Prize and the portrait on
> the postage stamp, and by cutting off that head,
> leaving the whole body lifeless? O treachery!

And out of the muddy ashes of these our Indians rise the hippies, to set up their ceremonies.

But the Yippies are mad at Mobe. And the Motherfuckers have said that they're not coming to the Inauguration because their concern now is the strengthening and forming of affinities in the community.

Some of the Yippies are there and talk about disrupting the workshops because they are old-style bullshit. There is a young man who takes charge of the meeting in a very authoritative tone. He means not to and yet doesn't quite know how. He wears an army jacket and has short hair. He sits on a chair in the middle and tells the plot of the play. As a ritual mode it may be fine, but it should be a rite, and not a theatre piece.

> Except insofar as Abbie Free says all
> Demonstrations/Lives/Actions/are now Theatre.

The Motherfuckers come in. They stand around and mumble to each other while this super-straight radical is telling the play to us. Carol, one of the Motherfuckers, sits

down in the middle and nurses her baby, Kotch. The chairman asks for silence.
The Motherfuckers say that one of their guys is in jail and they're trying to raise seventy-five dollars' bail. The chairman accuses them of deliberately coming here to break up the meeting. The Motherfuckers tell him to get off his ass. He is still sitting on a chair, and he's the only one sitting on a chair. He gets up.
He tells them they're disrupting the movement. They tell him he doesn't know how to make peace because he doesn't know how to talk to his own brother. When we leave to go to the theatre they're making a pitch for the bail money.

Steve Ben Israel and several other members of the company are planning to fly to Washington from Wisconsin to be there in the action. They'll meet us again in Iowa or the next stop.

Too little solidarity, but there *is* a unifying force.

We leave early to visit Carol Berger, who is at the hospital to have a major operation on Monday morning, just after we have left for Chicago.*
She is stunned and beautiful, surrounding her hospital bed with colored scarfs and peacock feathers, and fixing colored gels over the bed lights. She sits in queenly sorrow,

* Carol recovered from this operation and toured with us until September, 1969, when the Company decided to divide into smaller groups for greater effectiveness. Carol, her husband William Berger, and several members of the company were arrested on drug charges in Positano, Italy, in August, 1970, and taken to jail in Naples. On October 13, 1970, after two and a half months of imprisonment, and after four days of pleading for medical attention, Carol Berger died on the operating table of the prison hospital. Two days later twelve of the original fourteen arrested were released. The charges against Carol were never proven or even tried.

her embroidered robes covering her hospital gown.
Everyone in the company gives her a token, their favorite fetish or jewel, whatever is most potent for each. I lend her my peace symbol, which she puts on over dozens of other chains and necklaces.
She is uncannily cheerful. Everyone is cheerful with her and the whole company trembles.
The night before, from the stage of Hunter College where we played *Paradise,* in the scene in which we say that the heart regulates the circulation of the blood, we appealed to the audience for blood donors for her.
There has been a critical blood shortage because of the flu epidemic and the blood banks are empty. They ask for many pints of blood for Carol's operation. The company has few members who are not struck down by flu; the audience is responsive.

On the morning of the departure for Chicago, the bus stops at the hospital and everyone who can, gives blood, and the line is long for Carol Berger.
Many of the students from the audience who missed her performance in *Paradise* come to give her their blood. She talks with them. She is brave.

She asks everyone to take a head trip with her for support during the hours of the operation.
It's hard to get news on the road. Sunday night we are in a motel near Carlisle, Pennsylvania, and Monday night we are as far as a snowbound motel in Ohio. We phone New York. The hospital says she's doing well.

JANUARY 7, 1969:

In Chicago we play at the university, in Mandel Hall. For *Mysteries, Antigone,* and *Frankenstein* the audience is pretty square, though good enough. Abe Peck, the editor of the *Seed,* the local underground paper, says that the freaks don't come to the university or to Mandel Hall, but by the time we play *Paradise* there are plenty of those he calls "freaks."

We live in a large hotel by the lake, the Shoreland, and frozen Lake Michigan fronts the windows on both sides. It is the setting for the love-hate scene between Mary and Shlink in *The Jungle of Cities.* How Julian and I loved to play that scene, with its lurid description of the sexual landscape. Now pruned and frozen, but those trees, as Brecht says, do drip.
We see this and the theatre. It's too cold to do more.

There seems to be a frozen stillness in the movement too, as if those terrible events of the convention could not have taken place here.
They say that Paris too is without action.

JANUARY 12, 1969:

Before the *Paradise* performance we talk with Abe Peck, some of the political activists, and Alderman Deprées, who's a political opponent of Mayor Daley. He speaks in well-considered political tones to us, making constructive suggestions.

Jenny, having changed her mind again, flies in from Morocco to rejoin the company.
Before the performance: Under the stage we watch a TV presentation of Grotowski's *Akropolis*.

JANUARY 16, 1969:

From Chicago to Madison.
In Madison the theatre turns out to be unlicensed. The choice is presented to us of going to play there in defiance of the law (the cops say they'll bust an unlicensed performance immediately) or of going to a church outside Madison called the Unitarian Meeting House, designed by Frank Lloyd Wright.
Morris Edelson, the activist who made the arrangements, including the neglected license, seems to feel we should risk arrest.
But the company, gathered together in Mary Mary's room for a line rehearsal, doesn't feel like going into a Wisconsin jail for the night or the weekend, because it would bargain too small a point for our liberty.
No point is small. To say: There should be no licenses—well enough, but we want to choose the useful moment.
We play in the Unitarian church, in the angular architecture, under the cracked ceilings, and in the middle of the playing area, a large puddle formed by the melting snow seeping in under the glass walls across the heated cement floor of Frank Lloyd Wright's architectural masterpiece.

JANUARY 21, 1969:

The Big Pageant.
Nixon's Administration promises to be a Big Show. This man's pseudo-modesty is the greatest sham of all. He, more than any politician going, would like to be a Caesar.
The television version begins with an Inauguration spectacle in which even the protesters are playing their little roles.
The "best part of the parade" is the passing of the armored presidential limousine in front of the contingent (not large) assembled with red flags, black flags, and Vietcong flags.
As the car approaches, the demonstrators are faced with three ranks of soldiers. The car, flanked by four secret-service men running alongside, is pelted with pennies, mud, paint-filled balloons.
One young woman protester is carried off, her feet in the air, dragged across the wide avenue.

At the ceremony a rabbi, a priest, and the head of the North and South American Greek Orthodox congregations deliver invocations. And Billy Graham asks God to endow N with "supernatural wisdom." When Graham speaks all the ladies of the presidential party go into trancelike states. The camera pans along these Roman matron faces rapt. None wear fur coats. All wear similar coats with fur collars and plain round hats: classical modesty is the theme. Nixon's speech is pseudo-noble in tone:

> "Our destiny offers us not the cup of despair, but the chalice of . . ."

JANUARY 22, 1969:

As we play Lawrence University in Appleton, Wisconsin, and Iowa University in Iowa City, Iowa, the news brings reports of uprisings in Berkeley and in Barcelona, in Tokyo, Madrid, and San Francisco.

Everywhere there are small groups and quietly simmering activity, even in the inactive places.

Garrick hears us plan the Madison, Wisconsin, *Paradise* and reminds us that this is the school which a year ago demonstrated against the Dow Chemical recruiters, and they have known broken heads and Mace.

JANUARY 23, 1969:

When we reached Iowa City we heard news that Abe, the editor of the *Seed,* has been busted for obscenity, the result of a cartoon drawing in the paper.

In Iowa City a small group campaigns for "Free Theatre for Free People."

They walked unpaying into a concert in the same hall where we are playing and they were busted and Maced. A man and a woman stop us in the cafeteria to tell us they will come in free for our shows and we offer all possible cooperation.

They attend and enter our performances unmolested and take up a collection for The Living Theatre; it's generous and includes a Chilean half-peso note.

In the lounge there is a notice posted in a glass case: "Pot Bust This Week. Stay Clean." But the longhaired are still outnumbered.

A bunch of shorthaired students put on a kind of embarrassed show, intended, I'm sure, not for us, but for each other. "Hey, man, look at that! Wow, did you ever see anything like it?" "It's Jesus Ker-ist." I note how we disquiet them in public, while any one of them, if we encountered him alone, would probably talk to us with friendly curiosity. But we are strangers, and an easy mark, and not in one place long enough for any but the most meager confrontation.

Throughout the sense of "no revolution here," there persists the sense that they would rally quickly if the revolutionary time announced its alternatives.

JANUARY 24, 1969:

When we return to Chicago, driving through snow and ice, Steve tells us about Washington with what I interpret as a forced-optimistic attitude. Jerry Rubin, Abbie, Allen didn't go, nor did the Motherfuckers. There were Rennie Davis and Dave Dellinger, who spoke of "affinity groups," and Steve, who spoke to a thousand people about starting the productive side of revolutionary living now, and there was some useful gathering of forces.

The company is paranoid about Chicago.
Some people want to find rooms outside the city, because they are afraid on the streets of Chicago because of the cops.

Tonight we play *Paradise* in the Auditorium Theatre, which is sold out—all four thousand seats—and that despite the refusal of the *Chicago Tribune* and the *Chicago American* to accept advertisements because they found the play objectionable.

When we get to the Auditorium Theatre, past the front entrance jammed with hundreds of young people in the five-degree wind frost trying to get in, there's a lawyer, Frank Oliver—who is, they say, a friend to man—warning us all about getting busted.
And then there's the Old Man of Chicago.
He has a warrant out for Julian's arrest. The lawyer says there are two men here to serve this warrant.

> Does that mean cops, to arrest him?
> Or a summons server giving him notice to appear in court?

That's the kind of preparation for *Paradise* that actors get outside the Gates of Eden.

"This is Chicago," says the lawyer, sinister, yet somehow saying it proudly.

We speculate about why they would make such a foolish choice as to try to bust Julian during a performance.

It seems like asking for lots of trouble and lots of publicity.

> That's an actor's preparation for Paradise.

A dozen flash bulbs as Julian emerges from the dressing room.

We figured they might try during the Guerrilla Theatre Rite; plans are that:

1. Julian stay near the stage.
2. We all work on making it nonviolent.

It never happened. The fuzz hung around, and toward the end of the performance:

> Julian left the stage during a blackout, dressed and went walking in the freezing cold, finally found a hotel room at 830 Michigan Avenue.

A moment after he left, a reporter popped into the dressing room.

"I'm from the paper," he says, breathless, apparently from having just been out in the cold.

"And he got past the two cop cars on the corner so he's cool."

I'm flabbergasted at this television-performance behavior.

How did it come about

that peaceful Julian Beck almost gets busted on an assault charge?

Like this:

The Case of the Old Man of Chicago and Marge of Madison: In Chicago, Julian leaps on the Old Man with a love hug as he stands on the stage complaining that the Rite of Universal Intercourse is obscene. The Old Man falls to the ground charging assault . . . In Madison, Marge heckles, chides us for not playing free. Julian screams. "You can't live if you don't have money." He spumes. She cries, "Don't spit at me!" Julian raves: "I'm not spitting at you, I'm covering you with my body fluids!" She weeps hysterically. She had to be consoled for two hours by the whole cast as she sat in the dressing room weeping, "I feel like going out and killing myself." After several hours of soft talk and affection, she cools out. She's right about one thing: We ask the audience to say whatever they want but we don't warn them that they are going to be beleaguered for what they say.

Both Marge and the Old Man felt they had been physically assaulted, though they were not. Both reacted extremely. But both are failures from our point of view, one because it took two hours to get her out of her state of suffering, and even then not to Paradise, and the other because he called the cops.

> Most of the personal confrontations are the play's miraculous moments. Every night we have stories of victories, of how we turned someone's head from anger and disgust to pleasure and understanding.
>
> But along with our victories there are such failures as these two. We cite them and use them as examples when we talk about our problems in this changing play.

These occasions are discussed and discussed again; it's getting to be like the great days of The Brig, when we'd rap into the night after performances about what it was about, how it felt, why it mattered.

JANUARY 31, 1969:

Through a snowstorm with travelers' warnings all the way, we drive from Chicago to Kansas City, Kansas, an unpretentious town across the river from the more metropolitan Kansas City, Missouri.

We play in the Soldiers and Sailors Memorial, a pompous building inscribed with noble warlike sayings. The *Paradise* audience is enthusiastic and naïve. They jump up and down at the notion of "revolution," and shout "Freedom" and dance a little, and mention the presence of an unusual number of police. There are several discussions about whether they should or would bust us, though I don't know for what. Good spirits, no politics, no dynamics.

Meanwhile we hear word: The Panthers in Kansas City are stalking the city hall.
In Chicago the administration building of the university is occupied.
Is that the first one that's happened right after we were there?
Nanterre? (We played there in December 1967. Among the participants in the *Mysteries:* D. Cohn-Bendit.)

The company meets at the request of Steve Ben Israel in Rufus' room:
To talk of Politics, Paradise, Personal Problems.
The children: How to guide them into a community?
What about their aggressiveness, what about their carrying on in the theatres during performances?
The psychological-trip effects of the subject matter of *Frankenstein* or the Plague scene in the eyes of a seven-year-old.

> When they know what we mean by it they are ready to see it.

FEBRUARY 6, 1969:

The West.
It's so self-consciously Western. I had expected a "naturalness" maybe even a naturalism. The people are

extremely unarmored. There is this phony theatrical aggressiveness everywhere. The bumper stickers say:

"America. Love It or Leave It."

"When guns are outlawed only outlaws will have guns."

Kansas: flat, depressing farmlands on either side of the road. Cattle: Colorado: first like Kansas, then it gets wilder, serer, spectacular; mountains, red rocks.

Ft. Collins: *Antigone*.
Boulder, Colorado: *Frankenstein, Paradise*.

The Wind River Indian Reservation: the road leads across wastelands. An Indian store where they sell beaded belts and moccasins. The pretty saleswoman and her ten-year-old brother or son are the only Indians we see on the whole drive; no people, except that in Fort Wachicha, where the Indian woman guide is buried, there's a store across from the cemetery.
Uranium is mined here.

From Wyoming to Idaho, and there, on the other side of the mountains, the nuclear reactor testing station, a huge expanse with nothing but the foreboding joshua trees on either side, far into the horizon. Theatrical; no, cinematic.

FEBRUARY 9, 1969:

We stay overnight in a little place called Arco, in Idaho.

On its main street on the electric-company building a big

sign announces that this is the first city in the world to be completely lit and powered by atomic energy.

A plain place, hardly a town. Arco is in no way extraordinary.
I look at the light meter outside the motel. It's an ordinary light meter.
Of course, I know it couldn't be any different and that the apparatus that is different is far away from the light meter, but that is just what seems so wrong. That the new technology should make no difference. That it is the same world, that the status quo is so rigid that the only way a new source of power is used is not in a new way but to empower the old way.

FEBRUARY 16, 1969:

From Idaho to Oregon: snow, mist, the Columbia River.
In Portland, Oregon, is Reed College. The hippest, according to Garrick: the one where he expects most from the confrontation of the school and The Living Theatre Company.

The Reed students are affectedly sloppy and look very good.
We play *Mysteries* and *Paradise* and *Antigone* for them.
I didn't see *Paradise* at Reed. I played through the *Mysteries* and *Antigone* in the throes of the flu.
On the nights of the *Mysteries* and *Antigone* there was a sense of not knowing where to go with these students.

Not Garrick's friends: They sit in their pad and talk about

how to make a better world and they know life style alone is not enough.
Of course they feel thwarted.

I ask those who complain:
"Don't you think all revolutionaries feel thwarted all the time till the moment of the final action?"
"And when is that?"

At *Paradise* Garrick was astonished at the apolitical and for the most part frivolous responses of his fellow students. Because it has been too easy for them it is not really revolution.
Is there a contradiction in this? Or is "the revolution" intrinsically a process and not the product of a process? Here are students whose easiest vocabulary is "the revolution," and each one of whom must have some concept of what he means by that.
These are smart people. They know what happened in May in France as history. They study it, and a few months ago is like a few years ago because it's already studied as curriculum and traditionalized.
And they know all about what happened to the peace movement and all about the new violence.

Garrick says he wants to quit school. Karen says she's intended to quit school anyway.
At Garrick's and Karen's house they sit and talk of plans. Windy Simons is there, appearing mysteriously as he always does, sent by a friend of a friend, talking about rock groups and revolution. Very tender people—they don't argue with each other, but regret that they sometimes have to disagree, because they really want to be in Paradise every moment of the time.

There are only a few things they are sure of: they are for

peace, for honesty, for deeper human encounters; they are without personal material ambition: they want to live romantic, beautiful, useful lives. They don't know what to do.

Garrick talks of voyages to Africa, and of making a film with Karen, and of working to create a free school.
Garrick and Karen talk about organizing a small guerrilla theatre troupe at Reed.

FEBRUARY 18, 1969:

Garrick drives us to Ashland, but then he's too sick with flu to come to the performance at the University of Southern Oregon.
At a roadside café an angry drunk walks over to Garrick and asks him to come outside (to fight). "No," says Garrick, "I love you."
"You doan love me," says the man, coming at him.
"Yes I do," says Garrick, trying to talk directly, and the man walks away.
He feels it's a chance you take; he's very peaceful.

After the show we make our farewells. Garrick and Karen are coming to Europe. Their plans are all vague, but they are coming to Europe.

From Oregon to California.

It has a mystique, this land California, maybe left over from the Spanish mystique of earlier days.
Everything in California is very loaded.
As in a dream, when a certain scene seems deeply significant but you don't know why.

The cities, which look like roads lined with gas stations, mar the spectacular scenery. In Berkeley we live on a long blank avenue in a bleak hotel called the Shattuck.
Up the hill is the tree-enclosed campus of strike-torn Berkeley.

The city is full of ecstasy people and students. The students are very fierce-looking, dressed like guerrillas and heavily bearded, bundled in scarfs, caps, and heavy war-surplus jackets, not because it's so cold, but one gets cold after many hours on the streets.
The ecstasy people are on the other hand extremely classical in their behavior; they favor silences over lots of talk.
They are trying to shove the plastic op art into its puny perspective by the grandeur of beauty, which should overwhelm it.
They want to seduce the world to peace.
Which isn't the worst way.

They find fault with the "political" people.
They consider their life exemplary, and their experiments highly political in the best sense, and they want no lesser sense.
They feel the social responsibility, but they are more resigned to the length of the trip needed to bring help (to the screaming in pain) than are those who are out in the streets shouting Freedom Now.

When we arrive in Berkeley we meet two old friends, Michael Itkin and Allan Hoffman.

They are as clearly defined as figures in a tapestry:

> *1962:*
> Two pacifists, both beautiful and far-out.

Committing daring and pure acts of civil disobedience in the best Gandhian sense. Jailed with us, singing with us, and part of the story of our lives.

Years later:
Allan won over to the desperate persuasion of violence as a necessary good.
Michael, standing above the latest trend, preaching peace on the battlefields.

Michael: He is richer in his faith. He stages public ceremonies of great beauty with eloquent texts. And his adherence to the purity of pacifist religion is unwavering.

Allan Hoffman: He writes rabid poetry about vengeance though he is in his personal manner extremely gentle. A full beard makes his face soft and fatherly. He has a small blond son and a quiet, insistent manner. When he speaks of arming the people I imagine that his voice wavers. At the Times Square riot/when Kennedy resumed nuclear tests/ he sat down in front of charging police horses and stopped the charge with pure Gandhian zap.

The two pacifists, poet and priest, both illegitimate.
One turned to the advocacy of violence.
Both sober and somber.
They are not ecstasy people, both are revolutionary.

Here, too, is Diane di Prima, "former pacifist," now writing poems about guns and bloodshed called *Revolutionary Letters*. And her daughter; both of them in black velvet robes.
I find them and Alan Marlowe in the middle of the stage during the setup for *Frankenstein*.
Diane talks especially about her two younger children, born only fourteen months apart, one Alan's and one LeRoi

Jones', and how they are inseparable and devoted to each other.
It is her Peace.

After the *Mysteries* at Berkeley, we visit the Floating Lotus. It is a theatre commune filled with ecstatic realities. They perform an opera on a mystical theme. They dance and make music that isn't jazz-rock derived. It's getting very beautiful.
Pan-ethnic. Beardsley. Wagnerian in the pagan sense; accepts all creeds as if they were pure by assuming their innate purity; retreats from Campbell's soup.
Out of Zero. Back to the next world.
Conches and strange horns and soft percussions.
And whistling.

Michael Smith is there; he has written a book called *Theatre Trip*. He and Johnny Dodd are leaving for Europe to tour with the La Mama Troupe.
In the beautiful Floating Lotus room there is an altar, and we three sit under it, behind a fringe, and smoke and watch the dancers.

FEBRUARY 19, 1969:

Berkeley, California.
Ash Wednesday with tear gas.
The company is affected in a curious way by the battle down the street.
I flip out at Carl for the stubborn streak of militance at which he draws his line, not out of despair of alternatives but out of a stubborn attachment to the socialist revolution

as a continuous battle in which he is determined to play a role in keeping with certain old-fashioned ideas.
I accuse him bitterly of heartlessness.
He lets me rave.
"I knew this would happen to you in San Francisco," he says.

Some of the company go to the campus and return with the smell of tear gas and strong mixed feelings about what they saw.

I see everything politically much more clearly.
The place to be a pacifist is, in spite of everything, on the battlefield, and this battlefield, Kurushetra, Gandhi showed us, is in the heart, and it becomes even clearer:

> There is a Vietnam of the heart
> and a Vietnam of the planet.
> In the Vietnam of the heart we fight like hell;
> but on the earth we encounter our fellow.

I say I should go out and walk between the lines of cops and students and Carl says,

> "And cause bloodshed over your beaten body."

The television shows the two lines, and the tear-gas bombs thrown with a wide tail of white smoke.
And the students pick them up in burnt hands and toss them back.
The police wear gruesome gas masks and look like an expressionist play by Georg Kaiser.

I fly into a fierce rage about all the pussyfooting around the peace politics.

While everyone is still trembling with emotion: that's the time to stop the deception.

The militants lie about their readiness to engage in killing.
The pacifists lie about their acceptance of the alternative to killing.
Everybody gets polite like politicians.

Let the wind blow through, more openness.
There *is* peace with dishonor.
But there is no honor without peace.

The one whose pain cries out in his wickedness and in his infliction of suffering: he is especially our concern and our brother.

Otherwise there is no revolution; the victims on both sides belong to love, or to nothing.

Expedience! Always the same cry:

> What else can we do?
> What else can the Vietcong do?
> What else can the Jews do?
> What else can the tortured do, the torturers, the invaders, the defenders, the blacks, the whites, the babies, the workers, the soldiers, the students, the cops, the revolutionaries, the fascists?

For years I have been dazed by the magnitude of the problem and here is the cold ice of it.
(It is like having cold water poured on in the midst of hot hysteria: a sense of shock, and then of "coming to." A question—"Where am I?" and then a realization of where I am.)

My blood boils (under impact of the ice) and I am carried away by a feverish desire to clarify for others what has become clear to me.

Delineation: I see a necessity for saying I am here and you are there; you are here and I am there. Here we stand together, and here we stand separately. Stop pussyfooting.

> (I've been pussyfooting: I pussyfooted with the Motherfuckers and I pussyfooted with the White Panthers.)

Everybody's for a better world: protester, policeman, Panther, pacifist, patriot.

> P4U, P4ME
> Inundate the plazas of the world
> Knee deep in urine
> And odor of earth's diaper rash.
> Swim home in the waste products,
> Get out of the pisspot: don't
> Make waves. Fly.

The myth of the broad base is a bitch goddess.
Of course we will all overcome tyranny together.
Of course we know the Black Panthers are our soul brothers in the fight for liberation.

But the revolution is beyond that.
The revolution has come to that point where we have to say:

> "Here, my brother, I differ with you."

You can toss all the mystical ideologies together, as many are doing, to evolve a great pantheism, be a Buddhist, a Catholic, or a Zen Jew, or form a new sect, or be a Mithradite. Bake a great religion cake with all the images and all the names engraved on its wafers.
But you can't do that in politics.

You can't be a pacifist Panther. Yet I see some who call themselves pacifists wearing the emblem of the White

Panther. And when asked why, they do not know how to answer.

There is a young man here who stood between
the contending lines of cops and students and sang "We Shall Not Be Moved," and asked others to join him in the singing.
He was busted for inciting to riot.

My blood still boiling, I talk to Michael Smith a long time at lunch. He has been staying with Diane di Prima and Alan Marlowe and I ask him about Diane's defense of violence.
He says she thinks it's exciting. He seems to be put off by her penchant for excitement, but perhaps, I imagine, he's only coming on to me. Pussyfooting.

No one wants to hear my outbursts, so people pussyfoot around me. Michael Smith, in his book *Theatre Trip* (about a third of which concerns his visit with The Living Theatre in Europe), does not speak of the moral and political issues that concern us and are so much the subject matter of our speech: instead he speaks of life style and art style.

On the setup of *Frankenstein* I meet Super Joel, the superman of the canyon where two hundred ecstasy people live joyous and armed.
He has spread a feast of food on the stage floor in front of the *Frankenstein* structure.
"I went to XXXXXXXXXXXXXXXXXXXXXXXXXXX
XXXXXXXXXXXXXXXXXXXXXXXXXXXXXXXXX
XXXX so I bought a feast for The Living Theatre."
I don't say anything. I eat.
Later I catch him and talk, still feverish.

Michael Smith asks if Julian or I would do a preface to his book.

FEBRUARY 20, 1969:

We drive by the Berkeley campus, where a noisy picketing is taking place. It looks crowded but calm.

I am still trembling with the reaction to the violence.
And the Chinese New Year's firecrackers make me crazy with their echoes of deadly explosions.
I have a fever, probably the flu again.

A violent scene breaks out at Berkeley. The students and cops play a holding game with tear gas and advances and retreats, all teasing, dangerous, and inciting the heart to violence if not the hand—yet.

I rave in the dressing room. I plead for direct statements. I'm too sick to play, and between the fever and the rage I collapse after one last tirade about the violence, and lie down nauseous and shivering on the dressing-room table. When the Berkeley *Paradise* began, the audience had already begun its play. They came in off the arena on the campus; their theatre is the confrontation with the cops. All they had in them now was to dance. They were all doing their thing on stage, in the aisles, in the balcony. One by one exhausted actors staggered into the dressing rooms panting. "They really have us." "We can't get through to them." "They don't hear us." *"Je n'ai pas le droit"* is crowded out by the big party.

One scene after another goes down without a breakthrough.
Sick and exhausted and full of feeling, I lie there in the dressing room.
Super Joel comes in and tells of the wonderful community in the canyon and how they all built their houses, and how ecstatic their lives are. Now the police are coming to close them down.
Though they "legally own" the land—that is, they paid money for it—it seems they have no indoor toilets, and that's against the sanitary code, and besides, the water company wants the land.
He puts The Living Theatre down because of what's happening on stage, as though we don't appreciate the ardor of the ecstasy people.
He is one of the free spirits, but while he assumes the attitudes of the intellectual

> /he frequently says "You know what's wrong with The Living Theatre, it's . . ." etc./,

he doesn't think through. He skims across the ideas and lets easiest choices snap him up. He's beautifully communitarian, gentle of philosophy, over-energetic.
But he supports the violence, and when asked he says, "Sure it's wrong, I know that only peace can make peace, but what the hell."

The theatre is filled with uniformed firemen because someone at the *Paradise* party pulled an alarm. They come with axes and wearing raincoats. Everyone makes fun of them. They are presumed to be the allies of the police. People are rude to them.

The play ends at the Fifth Rung. The theatre is not in the streets.

We file out between the flashing lights of the fire engines that surround the building. There is a midnight curfew. Nobody is together enough to even suggest defying it. Super Joel wants us to lead the audience out the backstage scenery entrance, which fronts on the police station. Julian opens the back doors of the theatre but nobody chooses to make this the time to be hit on the head. Super Joel says we're finks. It's hard for people to understand how after a couple of such encounters they become feeble and meaningless until the time comes, the real call to say:

"Here I am."

The financial scene in New York degenerates. The debts mount. Right through the Midwest we still had full houses and here we do not. The top-heavy bureaucracy of the Radical Theatre Repertory can't be supported by The Living Theatre, which has always earned just barely enough to support its members.

FEBRUARY 21, 1969:

Governor Reagan comes to Berkeley, the man who wants to use stronger measures. The students hold a quiet demonstration, but the streets are filled with National Guardsmen. Armed to the teeth, they are transported in cars.

As I go to visit a doctor a block from the hotel I come out of the house past a parking lot in which soldiers are loading the trunks of unmarked cars with arms. Carl points out that the gruesome object that I take to be a flame thrower is only a tear-gas gun. They load several cars with these objects. We don't stop long to observe as we and the cops make each other edgy.

At night we visit Timothy Leary. He is a much more groovy person than the press, including and especially the underground press, has led us to believe.
He is in a beautiful house, in a beautiful room. Below, seen through a glass wall, is San Francisco.
He is surrounded by beautiful young people, and he himself is soft and beautiful in a blue shirt.
When we come in Leary rises and embraces Julian, holding him close in a hug like an old old friend, though they had never met.
Leary mostly smiles. He speaks softly and is pleasant. He doesn't say too much and that's pleasant—less challenging at a first meeting than an outburst of all differences as if they were a display of weapons.
When I say something that Leary likes he turns to Julian and asks, "What sign is she?" and Julian says Gemini without comment, and I don't give my nasty antisuperstition speech, but add that Julian is too, and I don't say that I don't hold much with that line of thought.

Jenny is raving. She staggers up the narrow plank where a Buddha idol guards the door to Leary's house. She is playing out the confusion. "Where are we?" she asks again and again. She's taking the whole trip, she's going into limboland and the great void, and she may just wake up cooled, or she may take the long voyage. She says it's the long voyage, and the fear and trembling shake her. She feels some special relation to me: tells me I understand it all; wants my aid.
I think she'll make all the stages. And I'm not really afraid for her, but it's terrible to see her suffer.
Tim Leary the guru-guide does not notice her anguish.

I'd expected not to like Leary. But I like him very much.
Shari says, "The press has fucked up our heads about him. The same way it's fucked with The Living Theatre's 'image.' "

Steve Ben Israel planned to ask him about the "new energy sources" that are all around us.
But the atmosphere's too easygoing and friendly to talk of such serious problems and we leave, promising to return for a more profound talk.
Leary says he's planning to go to India, and Julian asks him about the thirty-year jail sentence that's hanging over his head. But Leary is sure that he won't be jailed.

FEBRUARY 22, 1969:

Among increasing financial pressures we try to leave San Francisco, but stay in a motel overnight to visit Ferlinghetti in the morning. The day is fraught with crises over money. We arrive at Ferlinghetti's with our baggage packed and baby in arms.
In his small office we sit on the floor and talk. He makes tea.
Claude Pélieu and Mary Beach are there. Some reading matter gets passed around: *OPAL-U.S.A.*, by Claude Pélieu, a long poem about the culture.
Liberty or Death, a publication by Mary Beach, dedicated to Guevara, Cohn-Bendit, and Julian Beck, among others; it is a pamphlet of revolutionary writings.
Pélieu is handsome in that fancy French manner.
Mary Beach fascinates Isha with her painted toenails.
We talk about the French revolution.

> *1966:*
> Every afternoon and all day Sunday the Italians standing around in the piazzas. Once in Reggio Emilia, on the Cathedral Square, I asked Carl, "What are they talking about all the time, so animatedly?" "The Resistance," he said. In other cities it might be "the war." But once you've been on the battlefield you never stop talking about it—and you feel especially close in speech and spirit to those who were there.

St. Crispin's Day. That was some St. Crispin's Day: May in France. We happy few who chanted "Nous sommes tous indésirables," talk it through again and again like war veterans.

Ferlinghetti shows us Jean-Jacques Lebel's book on Avignon. *Le Procès du Festival d'Avignon, Supermarché de la Culture*. A collection—very straight, very formal—of press cuttings and broadsides.

> *August, 1968:*
> In Geneva, right up to the day we left, Jean-Jacques working day and night; moving into our hotel, gleaning pages from my archive, editing, photocopying.

Now it's a book. I ask Pierre Biner if the public will read it; he says only the experts.

Ferlinghetti plays a tape of Allen Ginsberg chanting Blake's Songs. We all get high on that incredible sound.

Gianfranco visited Allen and brought a message: to stop smoking tobacco: a message from the deathtrip of A. G. to J. M. and J. B. through G. M. Delivered like a strategy note.

Ferlinghetti does not speak of politics. He speaks of how Allen recorded the tapes.
He asks about the *Life of the Theatre,* the book Julian's been working on for the last seven years which Ferlinghetti's *City Lights* is going to publish.
And other manuscripts.

FEBRUARY 25, 1969:

Packing and unpacking: from the Shattuck Hotel to the Flamingo Motel, and driving away from San Francisco to Los Angeles. I get an attack of nerves: Everybody's tense about Los Angeles anyway.

In the car Julian reads aloud the lead story in the *Los Angeles Times* about the Motherfuckers and the Crazies, and it notes that the peace movement and the revolutionary violent movement are separating. As if it had some immediate effect, my demand—split the movement—is not *my* demand but the historical imperative of the time. The reporter seems to be a good guy. He describes the fierce MFs with an understanding eye, and talks about each group—Mobe, Yippie, MF, and the smaller bands of street fighters called Crazies—and where they are at with peace and violence.
Peace and Violence; it is no longer a matter of War and Peace.

As we drive south it gets warm and green. Isha calls the Pacific Ocean "a bath."

Los Angeles too looks like a road with many gas stations.

At the Starlite Motel there is jungle greenery on the hill side of the motel, and on the other side a view of roads and freeways, and a huge neon display announcing the Great Western Exterminator Company.

Money crisis. Jenny raves but won't let go.
The *Mysteries* performance is not sold out. Financial fears.

There is Glenn Lewis, who is in charge of the Computer Center.
He says the machines don't interest him. When I ask if he thinks they can save the world, he says he fears that they may destroy it. He talks about why he is there. I ask how he keeps from doing evil things there; he says by refusing to work on any classified information. He's smart and wise and aware of what's going down. I want to talk to him at length, but when we drive to the motel to discharge a few passengers, intending to go on to eat with Glenn, there's a big scene in the motel. They ask whether we can pay our bill. We can. (We just got paid.) Carl says "Fuck" because all the rooms have been locked up till each bill is paid then and there, and the motel calls the cops because Carl said "Fuck."
And there we are in the parked car in the motel yard, surrounded by policemen while one by one the actors pay their bills.
And in that glowing atmosphere

> —with moments like the one when Odile was told she couldn't go upstairs to see her baby, and she became an Algerian woman—

I go to sleep, sitting in the car, avoiding the whole scene, and Glenn goes on home by cab.
And so we move again, this time into the town, to the Hotel Figueroa.

While we build the *Frankenstein* set,
floods fill the streets with mud.

On television news we see towns turned to rivers and the city's hillsides falling down around us; and juxtaposed to that, Nixon's TV trip to the heads of the states. Everyone talks of N as a middle-road conservative type. I think he wants to be the greatest personality since Alexander the Great. He's taking every step under the canny management of his ad agency. He's the big product and I think he's going to be "sensational."

Jenny raves: the War-for-Peace meemies have her too. "It was Stokely that did give me Gandhi to read and said —go hear Beck—and then came Makeba who does want to be Empress, and she did say, "Do it with guns."

Everybody talks about the apocalypse of California. As floods wash down the houses (the $50,000 houses, Carl points out) and the oil seeps up out of the sea, the storms destroy the marina, the roads are washed away. Everybody talks about "the Fault."
Super Joel said he built his house in the canyon right on the Fault line because he hoped to die in that cataclysm.

FEBRUARY 27, 1969:

At a party at Roy Walford's after the *Antigone* performance, Dean Stockwell explains: Edgar Cayce, that visionary charlatan, predicted that the Fault would break off April 1, this year—well, actually sometime between 1940–1970, but the "sages" narrowed it down to next month. And the

proximity of the day of doom prediction gives everyone the creeps.
Dean, being of Hollywood, wants to tape over the Fault line with Scotch tape.
When we started *Antigone* at 9:00 P.M. there were earth tremors in West Los Angeles.

At this party too is Harold Norse, who is beautiful and knows where it's at, and bewails the loss of literature in the new world. He lives like a poet, always as someone's guest. We talk about Richard, who loved him so and was a fervent young musician. Now Richard works in a Madison Avenue ad agency and is content with his life. He says he can't write music. He enjoys the gay bars. How does this happen? Richard did several years in Chillicothe for draft resistance in World War II and paid his dues out front. What do we want from him?

I'm tempted to believe that Jenny is right, that there is something apocalyptic about this California. Doom talk all around; it makes me think of the 1950s, when everybody was obsessed with atomic destruction. We recall with Harold Norse how he bought a house in Connecticut to "escape" the holocaust when we all were paranoid about nuclear annihilation. Now that seems so naïve. We laugh at our former lack of sophistication. On the other hand, legend tells us that this place has always seemed crazy (been crazy?).

FEBRUARY 28, 1969:

At the *Paradise* performance in Los Angeles there's a lot of hassle about money before the show begins, and everyone is uptight about fire laws and exits and the fire marshal saying only twenty people on the stage at one time, and the police threatening—

> "I'm Lieutenant So-and-so, Mr. Beck, and we don't want any trouble here tonight."
> Julian: "What trouble? There's no trouble."
> Rufus: "There'll be no trouble if you don't cause trouble."
> Lieutenant: "That one (pointing to Rufus). He seems out to make trouble. I want you to have a little talk with him, Mr. Beck."

Then there was the decision to close off the balconies. Then there was the policeman rushing up and down among the dressing rooms swearing that he smelled marijuana.

The audience, not politicized, got politicized by the situation. They did come up on stage and there wasn't anything the fireman could do that wouldn't have started real trouble.
And when the people in the balcony felt the restriction, The Children of Paradise lowered a rope and came down into the orchestra, evading the guards at the door, and a wild cry of liberation rose up, and everyone felt that the example of revolutionary protest was defined.

Forty police cars surrounded the building. The play proceeded in peace. The audience left exiting between rows of armed-to-the-teeth L. A. cops with walkie-talkies.

Great exhilaration. But I'm worried about the fact that

there was nothing the police could do but make real trouble. On the one hand we showed them effectively that the chaos they fear is not harmful or violent; on the other hand we keep pushing them, and is it or is it not violent to provoke a man to the edge of *his* violence tolerance? Gandhi dealt with this all his life, in all his writings. He would say that without *Ahimsa* (= Love the pig, he is the beloved murderous brother) it is violent. That is, pushing to the limit of the other's conscience is not violence when love-motivated and is violence when not love-motivated. Is that true? There's something missing in this argument. And I don't know what. It has to do with escalation, with, with, with . . .

> the heart of the problem. So close to the core that it has no words, no thoughts, nothing but vague (subliminal) conceptions on the one hand, and the most concrete actions on the other hand.

If it is clear to me personally, but I can't make it clear to my comrades, where am I? Outside the community? What is a person without a community? Alone.

Like the Biblical prophets, I want to rage against the corruption without ever being thereby any less one of the people.
Was Isaiah or Hosea not one of the Jews because he put them down so hard and so poetically?
Can't I be of the revolution and rail against its violence like a prophet against false gods?

Can a pacifist be "abandoned" by his comrades? Of course not, he goes on with what he has to do—that is, always making Peace—no matter what the shifting fashions, or for that matter the shifting "politics," around him are doing. It may break his heart, it may make his work harder, it may make him go further out to reach an understanding of those who fall prey to violence (i.e., despair).

Is violence despair?

Is violence always *only* despair?

MARCH 3, 1969:

And so once we had proved that it was a safe and peaceful performance in Los Angeles, they (the University of Southern California) cancelled all our future (two) performances on the legal pretext that we were violating the fire laws.

A letter is sent politely explaining. A check awaits us at the university offices which is barely enough to cover the room rents. We wait all day at the hotel (while the personnel shout: "Check-out time is 1:00 P.M.") to get the cash to pay for our rooms. And behind this harassment is the meeting at the university, where the rudeness and implacability of the bigwigs is appalling.
It brings down Carl and Julian.

Continuing discussion: Who are the bad guys? And what are their motives? Everything I hear about this is either so full of invective—

> "It's the fucking capitalists, it's the perverted generals"—

that it's senseless or so finky that it's not to be considered—

i.e., Rockefeller III writing: "In praise of the Revolutionaries" (sic) for the *Saturday Review.*

Tolstoi's "What Is Power?"

/A collective chimera?/

MARCH 4, 1969:

So we leave Los Angeles broke, and travel back to San Francisco, where, because there is a "community," we have arranged for free housing for everybody.

On the road Carl calls San Francisco to learn that the Internal Revenue Service has put a lien on the box office of the theatre and is holding all monies and bank accounts which hold monies for The Living Theatre. Feeling harassed, with no visible means of support, we arrive in San Francisco; the big bus is there already and has unloaded its passengers at one of those beautiful clean communal houses.

Food is being cooked, dozens of children are underfoot. A flute quartet, mother, son, and lovers, is being played in one room. A combination of excitement and calm.

We have been driven into our corner. We have been driven into our home, into our comumnity. Michael Itkin—holy cook—asks if anyone wants to help scrape vegetables, and Gene Gordon, vegetable-scraping-mystic-revolutionary, volunteers. I get into a thing about nonviolence with Allan Hoffman.

We go to stay in Lawrence Ferlinghetti's office, where there is no heat, but which has three rooms—office, bedroom, and kitchen. Julian and Isha and I on the floor of the bedroom on mattresses. Jenny and Suzanne on the floor of the office without mattresses. Carl on the small bed in the kitchen. Surrounded by a distracting amount of modern literature. Cold.

No sooner have we unloaded the car at Ferlinghetti's than we rush (no time to eat) to the Straight Theatre in Haight Ashbury.

A decrepit movie house with the seats removed. Three of the walls covered with screens on which some light changes are projected intermittently, a rope net suspended from the balcony to the orchestra on which energetic people climb for fun and practice. Half toy and half dream of guerrilla warfare in the suburbs.

Loud music, great stomp fests: circling: a little uncoordinated chanting. A thousand people.

No longer called hippies. They are called freaks. They aren't wearing flower clothes. They are wearing beautiful clothes or shabby clothes like the beats used to wear, but decorated with an extra scarf or shabby velvet vest or many declamatory buttons.

The Motherfuckers are here.
Lots of music and action. Everybody's working at joyous.

They aren't hippies and I note with surprise that they *aren't* young. Many are in their late twenties and there are lots of thirty-year-olds. They have a different set of scenes and experiences from those of the eighteen- and nineteen-year-old college students.
They are Hedonistic Communitarian Anarchist.

They are dancing. It isn't possible to do a play in the midst of this dominant activity. And why should we?

We do a rather good Mat Piece. Leaping into the middle of the dancers, and jogging around with them, The Living Theatre actors create a space in the middle of the dancing.

/Jenny described how in Morocco performers make space in the crowded markets./

They strip to their costumes and Rufus lies down and makes a sound.
About a third of the people gather in a circle around the actors. Another third notice and watch part of the time and go back to the dancing; the other third never really knows a scene is being played besides the spontaneous scene around them.

The concept of the Liberated Zone is great.
The concept (often said and written) that you are the Liberated Zone is even greater.

But to get together once a week, or three times a week, to dance is not yet community.
It could grow into more fruit than flower.
Or it could rot,

stay flowery, dance, and never bear the revolution.

There's this dumb-bunny selfishness that means to change the world with a spurious argument.
i.e. Because someone clever has found a way to sneak across a border without a passport, he feels that the problem of frontiers has been eliminated. It's as if the good example of a few smart-ass radical beauties could work the wonders for the war-torn and the starving and the jailed and the wage slaves. That the scene is about revolutionary outcry escapes them in their feelingless

notion that "we are beyond that." Who are "we"? The ones who are dying of starvation every second? They haven't found out how to live without money. Till *they* have, have I?

Here in the Straight Theatre they are dancing the Bacchus Dance while *Antigone* is being immured.

No, it is not that bad—underneath you can hear the Indians.

After this chaotic scene we go to Diane di Prima's beautiful house, with all Alan Marlowe's oriental grace.
Alan Marlowe's Alex and LeRoi Jones' Minnie drawing pictures.

They concentrate on meditation and violence.
And "living beautifully." Incredibly productive. Diane cooks and tends the kids, and is unruffled, hard-working, and beautiful. She gives us a copy of *Floating Bear,* which she has just finished stapling.
She has written a lot of new books and made translations of *Love Poems from the Middle Latin.*
A poem of LeRoi's is stapled to the wall.

MARCH 5, 1969:

Internal Revenue at the last moment lifts its lien, after Saul and the lawyer Jerry Ordover spend hours with papers and phones and negotiations.
At *Antigone,* another hard talk with Allan Hoffman.
Terrible talk about our old friends—comrades—who have swerved in various directions.
Especially Bayard Rustin:

Allan Hoffman and Michael Itkin get completely paranoid when they talk about Bayard—they agree on little else, but in their fear they bring incredible accusations against him.

Because he now works for the Establishment, they fear that all the years when he worked with such devotion for the peace movement he was really in the pay of the great opposing camp: and even worse and unspeakable thoughts cloud their talk . . .

I don't believe it.

I remember him singing "He's Got the Whole World in His Hands" in the church where we stopped in 1958 on one of the long peace marches on Washington.

Why not believe that he got scared by the violence and the threats of retaliation with violence and decided—even if mistakenly—that the best way to protect his people was to play politics?

Of course that's what they all do: Does that make him Adolf Hitler? Well, does it? Answer me.

And furthermore—

> "If I can't love Adolf Hitler I can't love anybody," said A. J. Muste.

And it was he, A. J., who worked beside Bayard all his long peace career, and guided him. Maybe the loss of A. J. was his final despair.

Every day the newspapers list the disturbances in the various schools, as if they were different battle fronts in a great war.

In the cartoons and in television humor the jokes are all

about the longhairs, the protest marchers, the revolutionaries, and the generation gap.
They are all designed to make the protesters look like idiots.
In the coffee shop on Grant and Columbus, where I go to have soup and bagels with Suzanne Sutton and Alice Einhorn, an English pacifist comes to our table to attack The Living Theatre for its trouble-rousing at a time when he believes the scene needs cooling out. We soon are friends. He is Garry Goodhill, an anarchist from way back, who says he no longer calls himself a revolutionary—for the past year—because the word has come to mean something else.
He's worked here in San Francisco, and because of the scene he's been in he has come to some singular conclusions:

> "The revolution is happening. Nothing can stop it. The work to be done is to calm people's fears, to reassure them so that they don't freak out under the impact of the changes."

Working here in San Francisco he sees freaking out as the big evil because anarchist concepts are already accepted here. Now whether or not this leads to violence depends on whether the freak-out is too crazed to support restructuring.

The local problem is the future problem.
In Krefeld and in Kansas City they still need to find out what's happening and what's possible.

Campus news: a student planting a bomb gets blinded and his hand mangled when it explodes prematurely.

MARCH 6, 1969:

The taxi driver who takes us to the *Frankenstein* performance is a playwright from Amsterdam who is saving money to drop out and live in the country.

MARCH 8, 1969:

At the *Paradise* performance we confront them again: Allan Hoffman is drawn into a long, anguishing, bitter talk by Bill Shari, who holds his hand and appeals to his reason. Allan answers in oblique parables from the Bhagavad Gita, and how Arjuna learned to kill. I asked Allan why he thought Gandhi recited this bloodthirsty poem every day. He said because Gandhi is full of shit—look at his sex prohibitions.

Every once in a while Allan's passion is roused and he jumps up and shouts—"You gotta kill them"—and all his gentleness is masked with this angry thing.

Rod Beere is newer at the argument and comes on very fierce. Allan, so much more sophisticated after—what? Ten years—in "the movement," and a poet at that, upsets him. Rod puts his face near Allan's and points a finger, itching to be violent.
"Look, see here, I want to slap your face. But I'm not; I'm not!" (Shaking with frustration, he shouts):
"I'm not going to slap your face, even though I want to—because I'm a pacifist, see!"

Even Allan was moved by the plainness of the argument and the demonstration.
Later Rod admits that it wasn't all peace. "But," he says, "at that moment I learned that I really am a pacifist."
For three days there are all-day conferences about the money and the boat tickets—especially the boat tickets, which we suddenly learn were not paid for and don't exist. Equity will pay them from the bond, but this takes days of hasseling long distance—with the ship's agency, Radical Repertory, lawyers, the union, etc. etc.

Backstage at *Paradise,* Super Joel boasts of his bust for a heinous act:
He put a cherry bomb covered with paint and wrapped in tinfoil in the laundromat owned by a John Bircher.
He says it would only cover the walls with paint when it explodes.

I start to scream.

And he says, "It's harmless, it's only a paint bomb."

I shout about Isha and other babies playing around the laundromat while the wash is waiting! Any baby will certainly pick up a ball of silver paper and in my high-strung way I describe what will happen then.

He boasts that the charge was reduced to malicious mischief. I'm sure my talk was dismissed as the raving of a hysterical mother.

I'm discouraged.
I can't afford to be. He also tells beautiful stories about his community and their idyllic life.

There are two *Paradise* performances, the second on a day of exhausting activity. To make some money for the financial crisis we did three performances on Saturday, March 8.

The first was a lecture demonstration at Mills College, in Oakland, and the eager-eyed students performed well when it came their turn to play the Rite of Guerrilla Theatre. And there were some good outbursts, all getting more and more positive.

The session was filmed by television, which followed our scene and their scene—and then as their cry of "I'm not allowed to take my clothes off" rises, a tiptoed exit by the actors leaves them to their own devices.

From Mills College we drive with the TV camera and sound men in the car—urging us by their presence to "say something interesting," which we don't do—to a television studio where we do two pieces from the *Mysteries,* the beginning and the end, for an invited TV audience. Super Joel comes in in an Uncle Sam hat.

The TV studio feeds us with a vegetarian buffet, but the straight staff treat us condescendingly.

Exhausted, we come to the second San Francisco *Paradise*. Michael McClure and Jim Morrison—poet and pop singer —do a great number on race relations in the Capetown scene with Rufus.

MARCH 9, 1969:

The next afternoon, Sunday, we are to give a free performance of *Mysteries* in the park. Many of our friends have gathered in the cold sunlight in the park at the end of Haight Street.

The children frolic.

A TV man wants to do an interview, but the children are throwing firecrackers and I panic and go to the playground with Isha.

All The Living Theatre children are on the swings and carrousels.
A pastoral air: goats and ducks and sheep in the playground.
Isha is delighted. "I like it. I like it," she shouts.

Meanwhile, over on the hillside, the actors are squabbling with the friends about the appropriateness of the "I'm-not-allowed-tos" for this audience. We feel it applies, they feel it doesn't.

Michael Itkin comes to the playground bringing me a leaflet put out by the commune that calls itself "Armed Love" and written by Allan Hoffman. I recognize the poetry.
It speaks of liberation and of guns.
It looks as if The Living Theatre is performing in support of guns to defend the community!

I flip very quietly. First I say, "Uh-huh."

The leaflet is to advertise a free performance the next night, at which it is supposed that the Straight Theatre will be "liberated." They want it to be open free one night a week. We agreed to do a piece of *Paradise,* or something else, but not for the purposes described in the leaflet.

The *Mysteries* in the park never takes place.

Michael Itkin asks about the word revolutionary. The trepidations that I've felt for a long time about using a word

LEAFLET:

We are the eye of revolution stoned out
    freaks of the unknown
Destroying and creating magicians
    of a new space
Time . . . New reality becoming environment
    transforming the landscape of concrete,
    into the Paradise of free lives
Gargantuan energy blasting thru the delusion
    of Amerika
Tearing away past & present
We are the life of man's future
Community of lovers--armed with drugs--
    magic--guns & sex
    We are the eye of revolution tribal
    culture
Armed with our lives
Merging bodies together in a new way
We are the one
Energy of emerging future
We are life & death together
We are the eye of revolution blown minds
Screaming singing stoned
We are seeds of future evolution
Snake dancing thru a world of images
New life energy racing across the planet
Spinning at the center of galactic storms
tearing down the ghetto of their minds

—Armed Love Commune

so loaded with violence trouble him. I explain that I've gone through lots of changes, and I've concluded that:

my position is the position of the Hebrew prophets

> /I beg to make a distinction: that is, in claiming this position I do not mean to claim any of the virtues of the great saints, only to take as exemplary their attitude toward their people./

who railed at the Jews for their abominations, and put them down as worse than the heathens.

"The Whore of Babylon," interjects Michael.

But never, not for a moment, did they dissociate themselves from their people. They never cut themselves off; they were very much their people. With them, and for them and of them.

So: I want to be of the revolutionaries and abominate their violence, support their struggle for liberation from tyrannies and oppression, and uphold the faith that freedom can be won without doing murder.

I want to rail at the revolutionaries for their abominations, and put them down as worse than the heathens, but never, not for a moment, do I want to dissociate myself from my people. I don't want to cut myself off.

The children play on the swings, the carrousel, the sliding pond.

Meanwhile Julian has a hard time with the comrades on the hillside, and comes back tense, to drive us to Diane di Prima's. She has invited us for a meal "after the performance."

In the car we talk about the leaflet. I ask Julian what he

proposes to do; he says he doesn't know yet, he's hardly read it. I angrily accuse him of putting off, and pussy-footing, and he righteously/and rightly/ gets mad at me and rails at me for putting everyone and everything down/ just when I was thinking of the holy prophets/and tells me angrily that I'm a bitch and in this mood we arrive at Diane di Prima's.

She is making collages. She shows us her first and her second collage; she is working on her third. The room is littered with beads and bright-colored papers. Alan Marlowe, the perfectionist, cleans up, even to scraping bits of glue off the floor.

We got right into it. I suppose I came in complaining about how I was brought down by all the talk of guns; and Diane was tough about it, sort of priding herself on a "hard-as-nails" attitude all out of keeping with her gentle nature. But Alan Marlowe flared up, much as Allan Hoffman had done in the dressing room; he strode about and worked himself up and said that those who impeded the revolution with their antiviolence would be hung and that I'd be hung and that he'd hang me.
He pointed a threatening finger to my nose and said, "And I'll enjoy it too, I'll love hanging you"—adding sadistically, "And you'll love it too, you'll enjoy being hung. . . ."

I can't say I was left unmoved by this grotesque suggestion. But I certainly was hurt.

I argued awhile and called it poetry. Not good poetry either, to say he'll hang me, but fanciful.

What an insane view of revolution—a revolution in which Alan Marlowe personally hangs Judith Malina.

God willing, it's only talk!
Julian comes in and cools things off.

We talk about India. Diane argues that the theory of many reincarnations somehow excuses the forcible termination of life. A kind of karmic apologia for killing.
"If I kill you," she says to Julian, "it will only speed you into your next incarnation."

Excuses of the Inquisitors.
And of the exploiters and tyrants who say, "Wait till the next world!"

This is what Alan Marlowe has derived from his meditations!
This is what he has learned in India!

> Ah, India, where the young people are marching to demand that India develop an atom bomb!
>
> > *Early 1960s:*
> > A meeting called by Bayard Rustin for the War Resisters League in Greenwich Village at which two Indians who had worked with Vinobha address us and defend the Indian military, and I ask them about Gandhi and they say,
> >
> > > "Can we believe he was only human like the rest of us? For him the divine way was possible, but it is not possible for us—we are human. Only once every two thousand years. . . ."

O Bapu!
O Lamb of God and Prince of Peace!
O All-merciful!

> Why does Thy Other Pillar shelter in its shadow such rigid strength and needless suffering?

The collage material is cleaned up and we go downstairs to a beautiful meal. The children burn some of their paintings in the fireplace. We sit on cushions around a low table. We talk of good things. They talk about the food communes and how they are arranging for free food for the community. They get surplus vegetables and fruit with slight damages directly from the farmers; they also arrange for organic (unpoisoned) food.
They talk a great deal about ecology.
I am reminded of the two essays that Murray Bookchin gave me a year ago in Paris—the one about the beautiful revolution that serves both our needs and our desires, and the other which was my first introduction to the revolutionary aspects of the ecological problem.
And of his venomous polemic against Paul Goodman's interpretation of the nonviolent tendencies among anarchists.

At that time it seemed strange that this altruistic social planner, this builder of communities, this restorer of the planet's resources, was so enraged at those who violently supported the existing system that he seemed ready not only to kill them, but even to kill those who advocated not killing them.

Our California friends all talk about ecology a great deal. They are glorious communitarians, both in planning and in example. They are filled with the need to rave in defense of violence.

I prefer to believe that none of them is filled with the need to commit violence, only the need to rave about it.

How strong is the influence of an individual voice?
And how much is the voice of the times?

I hear the same phrases. I suspect the same source.
I admire and perhaps overestimate Murray. For his libertarian analysis of the revolutionary problems, and for his travels, and for his thorough researches, and for his magazine *Anarchos,* and for his insistent approach to me and to Julian. He asks pertinent questions, sticks to the subject, gets my addresses of the Swedish, Dutch, etc., anarchists.

But then I get paranoid and imagine the whole pacifist anarchist movement becoming a movement for Armed Agricultural Anarchist Communes.
But that's only when I'm paranoid.

At Diane's table not one unpleasant word was spoken in the candlelight and firelight. We talked only of agriculture and ecology.

MARCH 10, 1969:

All day before the performance at the Straight Theatre we talk about what to do there.
My anger at the misleading leaflet cools when I realize that there's not much that can be done.
I went through all the changes about making non violence —or the split in the community between pacifists and fighters—the subject matter of a performance of *Paradise.*
But the notion of playing *Paradise* at all seemed more and more irrelevant.

The objection to the Rite of Guerrilla Theatre was discussed. They simply insist on taking the words literally instead of being part of the action. Paul Shippi comes to argue against the use of the Rite of Guerrilla Theatre. We can't seem to make clear what the scene means. Instead of uttering the outcry of frustration, they only hear the "words"—they who reject "the verbalizations." Shippi claims that the community is "beyond these problems," as if the community were not a part of the world which is very hung on these problems. They do not realize their relationship to the suffering world.
As Cain to Abel.
But by midmorning it's obvious that we're not going to do the Rite of Guerrilla Theatre, and many plans are discussed for scenes from *Paradise* and *Mysteries,* or a mélange of the two. The best suggestion is the Brig Dollar—which by its decibels will command attention—followed by a rap about nonviolence, followed by the Plague scene, to be performed on cue when anyone of us flips out or starts to rave.

Not till we are enroute to the theatre is this agreed on.

All day there are financial problems—Equity, the boat tickets, the New York office—and long negotiations that come to nothing but: there's no money for our boat tickets. In the midst of this crisis Mike McClure and Joanna McClure come to visit us and we sit around and talk lazily. They have brought Jim Morrison (of the Doors), who is very quiet and easygoing. We eat honey.

We talk about this and that:

> About the students and whether or not they have something "to teach us." /Mike thinks they haven't/.
> About *Paradise*.

> About how Mike doesn't like the word "political"; he prefers to say "biological"/which comes to the same thing if either word is regarded with the least seriousness/.
> About literature/only a little—highbrow taboo/.

Meanwhile the phone keeps interrupting. Everyone's gathered in the tiny kitchen—Carl, Julian and I and the three guests—because Jenny and Suzanne are sleeping on the floor of the office and the bedroom is empty so Isha can go to sleep. Julian talks on the phone about the desperate money matters, and Morrison, who says very little,
offers to help.
He'll send money.

Start packing.
Great confusion.
Great pressures.
Dozens of people all day in the tiny apartment. No heat.

We gather in the house on Haight Street where many of the actors are living to talk about what to do at the Straight Theatre.
Allan Hoffman sits beside me and asks, "Do you really think I wanted to lie? Do you think I deliberately wrote something that would attribute something to you that you don't approve of?
"I used some old material, a poem, from New York . . ."

And because I was not moved to anger/I like him/I was sardonic and quoted Jenny's grandfather, who said that

> the trouble with murder is
> that it can lead to stealing
> or even to lying.

And because he and others found this amusing and

laughed, so that this serious matter was being dismissed as a joke, I added

> /I now think very indelicately/that if he were willing to kill to further his cause, why should he not be willing to cheat or to lie?

Since he answered me seriously, I did not press him but respected his intentions.
For he said, "There's no room for that in the movement."
I could have argued. But why? I was trying to make a point about honor.

But I would have done better to exemplify it.
We decide on what to do for the night after some painful talk.

When we arrive at the theatre Allan is there giving out a new leaflet: in a polite usher's manner he says,
"Would you like a copy of our lies for the evening?"

I lose all interest in this silly quarrel.

After the Brig Dollar, the rap leads into general chaos. A few people talk, say groovy things. A small bunch of frantic young people say vehement things (kill the pigs, etc.), but more by rote than by rage.

A very loud and powerful speaker is a young blonde chap named Allen (another Allen), who speaks of the forming of communes and the need for independence from the System. He is a member of a group called Messiah's World Crusade. I understand the Messiah's name is Allen also. I have read their newspaper, romantic and passionate, pacifist and anarchist.
Others shout above the dancing crowd: "Speed kills."
The chaos becomes too generalized for us to do the Plague

piece; so we stay awhile and participate in the scene, which is, they say, the occupation of the Straight Theatre. "They" say nevertheless "they" will clear the theatre at 11:00 P.M.

When we leave they are still dancing. No one is willing to exert an orderly or ordering element, because no one wants to face the resistance to orderliness that the initial hope of anarchistic liberation entails.

The natural order will emerge.
We have all the clues. And the cues.
We wait for it, we can't guess it. We could but we don't.
Something is missing.
But it's rapidly coming at us.

A beautiful example:
We are standing in the lobby of the free and open Straight Theatre. It's crowded. Suddenly a lad of about fifteen, in a black leather jacket, runs in from the street through the center of our group, almost knocking us over.

Someone behind us says cool and loud, "It's the bulls, here they are."
Two police enter with night sticks in hand. They slow down because there are so many people. Their quarry is inside the theatre.
They look inside from the doors that lead to the aisles.
There are no more aisles; no seats; no theatre, just thousands of people (it seemed so).
Someone says to the police, very quietly, as if observing a sports event: "There's thousands of people in there."
The cops leave. They lost him.

Because there was a free space, and the doors were open, and there was a community inside which would certainly want to protect him—not with violence, but by their presence there where he could disappear among them—

> could disappear like Lao-tzu when at the end of his career he vanished *into* the people—

therefore he escaped the police.

What if they don't conduct meetings like the French students, but only dance and jump around?
They have provided a place for the fugitive.

At that moment, under that young man's feet there really was a liberated zone.

We leave San Francisco before we learn whether there will be free nights every Wednesday.

MARCH 13, 1969:

We leave the next day.
Jim Morrison gives us twenty-five hundred dollars.
Saves our skins.

We pack and travel south.
Because we want to go through Indian country.
To Arizona: in the Mohave Desert rocket pads and housing make silhouettes like Frankenstein's castle.

The radio says: school disruptions in Los Angeles.

MARCH 15, 1969:

We travel the long trip to Boston.
To Grand Canyon, where a group of Hopi Indians perform dances in the gift shop.
"Hello, folks," says the leader, and he lifts Isha onto a three-cornered leather stool.
They are a small group. I think a family. The store is small; the tourists crowd around.
The Indians wear full costumes for the Comanche Dance, the Eagle Dance, the Feather Dance, and the Hoop Dance.
They evoke strong feelings. One feels they are the remnants.
Isha is impressed by the smallest dancer, a boy of perhaps five, who dances with the skilled discipline of his elders.
We travel the painted Desert from Arizona to New Mexico.
We see the homes of the Navahos and the Hopi.
Round shacks of earth or wood (far apart from each other) on the immense plains. Everywhere the signs of poverty.

It is not now as it was then when these same wooden houses or round mud shacks stood on a plain where there were buffalo.
With big game these were beautiful houses and now they are ugly. What is beautiful is beautiful only in context.
This vast wasteland, "given" to the Indian devoid of its natural inhabitants—the animals—is an insult to him.
We lunch in Gallup (at the Greyhound bus terminal), which bills itself as "The Indian Capital of the World."
Here are the town Indians and they move in a depressed way.
They are like the blacks thirty years ago—I remember them —stifled and shuffling and oppressed into a humble stance, with no realization of their beauty, sullen and angry or defensively submissive.
And now that's all gone. The blacks have the ardor of

their liberation in their steps, in their voices. Their eyes
flash, they move (indeed) like panthers. . . .
In the way they move they are already free.

But in the Indians there is only this sense of doom.
They are proud—but they feel no hope for their pride.
There is something fierce still: it could, like the black
man's downed spirit, be roused and activated.

But who is to say to them, "Open the roof to the rain!"
on their vast, fruitless, barren, waterless, gameless,
fowl-less, radioactively-poisoned, empty plains?

> Someone will rise up among them and tell them to join the revolution, to be the revolution. But he or she isn't here yet.*

We visit the Taos Pueblo. We register at the entrance to the village and pay a camera fee, and then walk around inside the plaza and the small passages around the three pueblos and among the smaller houses, as if in a living museum in which everyone is uncomfortably both observer and observed.

The Indians cover themselves in bright, cheap blankets, not Indian blankets but low-priced Sears, Roebuck blankets—plaids and boarding-house stripes. They wrap them around their heads. They go about their business: They fetch water in tin pails from the stream that runs through the center of the plaza; the old men just sit. A boy tries to sell us tamales but admits they are made with meat. Great friendliness, but every smiling greeting turns

* I did not know then that the Red Power Movement was already preparing to take revolutionary action. A year and eight months later the Indians occupied Alcatraz.

into a sale: of a beaded belt, or "Take a picture of me— one dollar!" The old men are all drunk.

Mud.

MARCH 17, 1969:

Through Oklahoma, the flat fields to Missouri, across Kentucky.

The experience of California is always with us, and the sense of the struggle.
The landscape's changes reflect everything back like a review of the tour.
The poverty of the aboriginal reality.
The poetry of the aboriginal reality.
The plastic landscape of the filling stations:

> The lotteries called "games" at every stop.
> Wiki Wiki dollars.

The pioneers with their nasty humor.
The pioneers with their cheerful friendliness.
The lack of art.
The loss of art.

> Those sad official statues.
> The coy kitsch of Forest Lawn.
> The municipal buildings in modern style.

And the good earth ("the unspoilable and untiring") spoiled and tired.
The national parks like cages: bits of nature in a zoo for

disappearing species.
The wasted planet.

MARCH 20, 1969:

On our eighth day in the car from California we reached Elizabethville, Kentucky, which is near Fort Knox. It also houses a museum of General Patton and of military armors. I learn this at the cashier's desk at the luncheonette, where they sell postcards of tanks, and on the obverse it says: "Spewing Deadly Napalm."

Isha wants to get out of the car. At every stop she fights not to go back. We all feel that way.

But in order to play *Mysteries* at a discothèque in Boston on schedule we have to drive through the night, arriving in Boston at 11:00 A.M.

> Flippy nerves:
> Steve Thompson says, "The Schmuck is in the lotus"
> From the German word for jewel.
> Jenny says, "The millennium has come."
> The headlines say that the Attorney General has learned that the campus riots were instigated by conspiracies and that the conspirators will be prosecuted.

Two Crazies come backstage after *Antigone*. It was they who disrupted a political science class with impertinent questions, calling themselves at that moment "The Students of Life."

And they took their clothes off in a laundromat in Harvard and put them in the washers and washed them, and as they were resisting arrest they said, "People think it strange if you take off your clothes—that proves it's a repressive society." And other work.
They have sober, childish, smiling faces. They are full of enthusiasm. They live in a small commune of eight people.
Danae Brooke, from London, writes "America needs you but Europe loves you."
Antigone in a discothèque.
With a uniformed policeman standing nervously and self-consciously on the stage area, setting the whole thing off like a stage set.

MARCH 21, 1969:

We arrive in New York exhausted—having driven from Boston with no time to eat—take Isha to West End Avenue to her grandma, unload the car, change into orange tights

/for colorful effect in anticipation of a drab evening/

to attend a Theatre of Ideas symposium on *Theatre or Therapy?*
This Theatre of Ideas is a long-time project of Shirley Broughton's. We know her from the old days at the Cherry Lane, where she helped with a benefit for The Living Theatre.
The Theatre of Ideas is a forum of intellectuals talking of this and that serious problem.

I read in the *Times* reports of Hannah Arendt's discussion of violence and other such events there.
The scene is the Friends' Meeting House, on Gramercy Park.
We meet friends: Paul Goodman, who looks unchanged for all that sorrow.
I do not dare mention his son's death to him. Warm embraces. Later his eyes fill with tears when he says to Julian that he can't speak of it yet.
Nat Hentoff and Bob Brustein are amiable. We sit on the floor and talk about who's going to talk first and about the title *Theatre or Therapy?*
Nat Hentoff introduces the speakers. The Canadian Broadcasting System was also there, with a great deal of gear. A full house.
A benefit for Theatre of Ideas, at ten dollars a seat; all occupied by writers, editors, teachers, psychologists, artists, and all kinds of highbrows.
Brustein talked earnestly about participation. About freedom and responsibility. The audience member cannot be a sublime artist, he contends.
It was a serious talk. He spoke in favor of an elite. And of the need of the elite to exclude the generality from becoming members of that elite, or enjoying all its privilege.
Paul spoke. Moderately. On the subject he had promised us when we were sitting on the floor.

His proposition is:
We are not in the historical situation of the Christians in the catacombs, but in the historical situation of the Protestant Reformation. It is not a civilization in cataclysm.

I think he is trying to cool it.

He's been on all those campuses. He feels it has to be put together. Maybe it's too frantic. It's hard to know what he's asking for. More common sense? There is something shocking about the conservatism of his viewpoint, even the scholarly presentation—though he has always been scholarly, and rightly prides himself.

> "I am Erasmus," he says, "but in some ways I'm better than Erasmus."

But I hear him through the ears of the company members who are hearing him for the first time and expect so much from him.
Lucid. Consolidating. Bringing together the information. Trying to locate our historical position.

> It is neither early Christian nor early Reformation—it is early postcomputer—and while there are plenty of historical analogies, it is unique.

Henry Howard heckles from the balcony: "Open the jails. "Why don't you talk about opening the jails?"
Paul says, "I always do."
Later I explain to Paul that Henry is really on trial, to be tried the next day, and he becomes much more sympathetic to the interruption. "But," he says, "Why didn't he say that?"
Paul is griped by the interruption but good-humored about it. After Paul speaks, I speak.
I don't say anything interesting. I defend the anarchist position. I defend the sublime artistic talent of the audience member.
Rufus interrupts me. Then Steve Ben Israel interrupts me. It soon and easily becomes a *Paradise* riff-blowing on the subject of why these well-dressed intellectuals are there at ten dollars a head.

Before it even gets started Paul says to me, "That's spite."
And I agree that it has a strong element of spite in it but I think there are other phenomena too to be counted.
Paul says, "I'm going home. Right now."
(That's spiteful too.)
I urge him to stay. He leaves.
Julian and Steve Thompson run after him in the lobby to urge him to stay.
He goes home.

Many scenes are played. There is a good deal of anger.
Nat Hentoff feels it's appropriate to the subject matter of the evening as a sort of lecture demonstration on *Theatre or Therapy*.
Shirley Broughton is outraged and speaks of calling the police.

I try to make a speech into the microphone about the scene before us. I propose a discussion about the scene as the scene is played out. I tell them not to be afraid.

But it's too late for any sort of form.

Norman Mailer comes storming up and tries to make a speech over the mayhem without a microphone, all his friends standing around saying, "You mustn't shout like that." And finally with a microphone he makes a characteristic speech. Many cheers.
He is well liked.
Richard Schechner tries to plead for a moment of silence but nobody listens.
John Simon hurls insults at Richard Schechner.
Shirley Broughton insists that Julian "order" his "people" to stop. He explains that he can't do that; a moment later he has joined in the scenes.

I see a mink coat flying across the room and I hear
Julian's voice loud.
I never get into it really. It's too aggressive for me. I'm really not more outraged at these people than I am all the time anyway, and I have a soft spot. . . .

Kept intelligentsia? Who isn't kept? Who isn't bought? Who doesn't eat the bread baked by slaves? Not one. If shouting in their ears will help, then shout. I feel rather benevolent about the whole thing, and I remain up on the dais, talking to people in all states of feeling about what is happening. Lots of people I haven't seen in five or six years come up and either praise the scene or play a scene of outrage with me. "You should be ashamed of yourself." "A disgrace." "You are doing a great disservice." Or "You can only do this because the people here are morally against calling the police." "That's right."

I try to reason with everybody.

Jimmy Tiroff, dressed up in velvets and using the name Olé, comes in and makes shocking proposals to Norman Mailer. There are dozens of far-out scenes.
Many people cry "fascists" at us and urge calling the police. The scenes go on till 2:00 A.M.
As we leave I express my regret to Shirley that she should be made unhappy, and though I assure her that we were not aware of what was going to happen, she's very skeptical about that and, though polite, very bitter toward us.
"They're bored," she says. "It's *so* boring."

That was the Theatre of Ideas.

MARCH 23, 1969:

Immediately the tempo of New York draws us in. The nervousness, the constant crisis. And the constant police paranoia.

There's the police at *Paradise.*
Then there's the news of Abbie's bust: lots of paranoia about the planting of stuff by the police, so that one is helpless even if clean (as if there remains that unquenchable hope in the fairness of the law—the bring-down that it's never a fair fight).
Abbie busted for guns and narcotics! His apartment busted while he was in court for the arraignment for the "Chicago Conspiracy." There's a picture in the papers of the bunch of them at the arraignment demonstration, and Dave Dellinger is holding his hand up in a clenched fist.

Why does he do that?*

Backstage at Brooklyn.
Jamie Malina—whom we had urged on when we met him at the first Bronx *Paradise,* naked, extrovert, political—is already into guerrilla theatre and he's joined the Motherfuckers. I say, "Bring them peace." "Sure." They value his services because he makes shoes. He doesn't mention to me especially that he teaches karate—because he's really peaceful.

Ciro and Jimmy Tiroff are far-out and create other-worldly scenes. Ciro pronounces oracles in one of the

* The change in the symbol of the American movement from the V sign to the clenched fist denoted not so much a change to violence as a change to militance; i.e., revolutionary activism as opposed to the tendency to "work through the system" by such methods as "electing peace candidates."

dressing rooms, which she calls "The Room of Truth." Members of the audience are brought backstage to listen to her enlightening words.

Richard Edelman in a crowded dressing room, where we can only talk amenities.

> *1954:*
> Amorous hero of the days when The Living Theatre plays still had "heroes":
>> The pure hero Arkenholtz of Strindberg's *Spook Sonata,* the lyric hero Orpheus of Cocteau's play.
>
> *1955:*
> Stylistic director of our production of *Phèdre* and of Claude Fredericks' *Idiot King.*

He's doing a new version of *The Miser,* he says. Nothing really about how much of the dream of ten years ago remains, and how much is fulfilled, and how much is always to be unfulfilled.
Igal Roodenko, who says goodbye as he has vowed to remain in the United States till the war ends. I wonder what that means. Igal is always so honorable.
Backstage at Brooklyn. Some people from Reed College give us a nude photograph of Garrick talking to the president of the college at a demonstration for increased personal liberties at a student-faculty meeting.*

* In March Garrick and fifteen students at Reed protested the rule against men and women staying overnight in each other's quarters. The faculty agreed to hear their complaint but they felt that a "theatrical" demonstration was the best argument, and so they took off their clothes and staged a "fuck-in." According to reports the action was for real. Then they argued (stark naked) with the faculty. (They lost.)

MARCH 24, 1969:

The Brooklyn *Paradise*s go well. The receptive audience tries to find forms. At the last performance I am personally challenged to take off all my clothes and I say I will if the audience member who challenges me will. We both undress while I talk about disarmament from the stage.

MARCH 30, 1969:

My last American performance is *Antigone:*
Isha is sick with the flu and I miss all the last *Frankenstein*s.
I stay with the baby while they play farewell to the U.S.A.

The last three days. Three visits: Joe Chaikin, Eric Bentley, Paul Goodman.

> *MARCH 27, 1969:*
>
> Joe had been sick. We kept getting bad news. Hospital. Fear of the need for heart surgery. He made a quick recovery and is resting at Jean-Claude van Itallie's house. We sit and schmoos about life and sickness and fear and our need for each other. About the theatre. We are all in the enigma. Joe wants to do resistance plays for high-school students. How to find a voice for this?
>
> We don't talk much about theatre. A little about his political scene but mostly about the kind of thing family people talk about.

And fear. And a great down. As if after a period of hope. Over.
Joe gives us a copy of Arendt's *Men in Dark Times.* We agree that this is a time when we read only for information. Joe is cheerful. In the operating room he longed for Jewish faces. He wanted amidst the strange proceedings—he was awake, alert, with a tube from his arm to his heart, which did not hurt but felt frightful—he wanted a few Jewish people around him.

A longing for home.

He lives in this strange corridor, moving constantly away from some longed-for home, and as it recedes, so the longing grows stronger.
Once he asked me if it ever stops hurting. And I said I thought it doesn't, but now I'm not sure. Maybe if we can't stop the pain, we can at least make it hurt differently for a time—so that we don't cry out so much, for instance.
He's safe, he says, as long as he doesn't get excited. It's hard to say good-by. We are late for dinner and the last *Antigone.*

MARCH 28, 1969:

Eric Bentley received us warmly for one who had rejected our work so harshly publicly. It was only formal because Eric himself is formal. He made tea and we sat around and talked of old times for a long time. And he told stories about Brecht.
How Charles Laughton, while playing Galileo, was horrified to hear that Brecht was a Communist, and disavowed him completely and because of this became involved in some very patriotic plays.

Later, when Brecht died, Laughton was sent an invitation to a memorial service and he telephoned the F.B.I.
F.B.I.: "Why are you calling us about this?"
Laughton: "I thought you might not want me to go."
The F.B.I. said he might go if he liked.
That kind of story.

And about Piscator.
He says it was on our (the school's) account that Brecht and Piscator had the bitter American fight that made irreparable the rift between them. That Brecht wanted famous stars and Piscator wanted his students at the Dramatic Workshop to perform *The Private Life of the Master Race.*

1945:
I remember the day the three men came to look at us. All of us sitting around the table of the Benton Room of the New School for Social Research, surrounded by murals of American Life by Thomas Hart Benton. They walked around the table looking at us as though it were a beauty contest, making little negative noises as they passed each of us, and glancing at one another. We never knew there was a quarrel about it: it was "they" who didn't want us to play. That day it was neither Brecht nor Piscator who fascinated me: the third man was Max Ernst, who was making a movie. From among us he picked a girl named Grace to play a sleeping beauty in Hans Richter's *Dreams That Money Can Buy*. To me it was he who was the great

man among them, the great painter. I was
heartbroken that he didn't notice me.
What did I know about Brecht?

Bentley says that Piscator did not go to East Berlin because he "wasn't a Communist," but it was my impression that he didn't go to East Berlin because Brecht did. That is, because he was not invited by the Cultural Ministry.

We talked about *Paradise Now*. When Julian outlined the structure, Eric said he liked what he was hearing more than what he saw. I believe it.
It comes to the old conversation we had years ago: that I want him to raise his arms to heaven and cry out, and he doesn't want to raise his arms to heaven and cry out. And I know he doesn't want to, and I still want to get him to do it.

I was relieved to be able to reassure
him that I hadn't singled out Eugene McCarthy as a "murderer" except insofar as we were all guilty of the killings and a man running for the job of Commander in Chief of the United States Armed Forces somewhat more so.
And he was glad we were so reasonable, and we talked about *Mysteries,* which he liked more, and then he made his pitch, which I think is an honorable pitch and a well-taken point, and shows him to be more actually political than I had thought him.
Since the war is now raging in Vietnam, he argues, no work is more important than to stop that war—and the war cannot be stopped by pressures from Europe; it can be stopped only by pressures here in the United States.
Therefore, he argues. The Living Theatre should stay in the United States, where the most immediate

work can be done. And he points out that "we, collectively," have already created a change, have opened the people's eyes to the war, aroused protests, indignation, and eventually could contribute to ending it.

He speaks with admirable feeling.

I am glad to sense his engagement. He's working very hard at his effort—to stop the war, and no doubt to aid the people directly victimized, and to awaken, if not totally assault, the culture.

He agrees that "they" would soon start another war, a "more popular" war (because they'll be more canny next time about the image).

That therefore some must work to stop the war and some must work for the world-wide revolution for peace. He gives us a copy of his "Man Is Man" record—the "Elephant Calf"—and we part with embraces.

MARCH 29, 1969:

Paul Goodman's house is sad, and we don't talk about Mattie except when Paul gives us a book of poems about him.

There's Daisy, who's six and a flowering blonde child, so much like the husky blonde Mattie who used to hang around during group sessions and during those long years of my psychoanalysis with Paul. There's George Dennison, Paul's protégé, grown wiser and arrogant: very talkative. Paul hasn't seen the plays, but we talk about the occurrence at the Theatre of Ideas. Paul feels the loss of dialogue. George complains about the level of the performances. He regards it as psychodrama, and it is that among other things. After a while Paul begins to complain about the students. He's been on three hundred and fifty campuses. His main bitch is that the young people aren't beautiful. We protest that they are. But he says he must trust his body and his body tells him that they are not beautiful.

Of course he likes a certain kind of toughness that is not fashionable now—except sometimes among certain militants—but even there it's not that kind of superior Horatio Alger that Paul loves.

He can't stand "the hate—all that hate coming out of their mouths."

And it's the ecstasy people who are the pacifists. And of course he would take offense at that gentle, bearded look with the soft eyes and the coming on tender expression that the ecstasy people cultivate, and in whom, for that matter, lies the hope of the world.

We all complain about the "dancing," about the "frittering away of the frenzy."

> Of clearing the stage:—"You're dancing over here where I'm trying to build a bookcase—"

Paul is down, and he's down on the students—and I suppose we are too.

> But it's Paul who's brought them to where they are, who said "anarchism" to them, who told them about sexual liberation. What does he expect? Gratitude?

He looks young. With his head as old as Erasmus. He shakes his head, as though he were old (he feels old—he obviously feels himself to be the old sage). He shakes his head and presses his lips together in resigned disgust.

> "You've got to define what you're saying more clearly.

"You've got to be precise—so precise
that you will be understood.
"So precise that you'll fail.
"I know about that kind of failure.
"I'm so precise, so defined that I'm rejected."

His latest book, he complains, is not even reviewed by any literary publications.
He is right to complain.

These three disheartened, discouraged, desperate American intellectuals—actor/director, writer, critic. Three people with diverse but pacifist commitments under great odds, all very down: Eric still hopeful of some amelioration by political action, therefore less pained. Therefore less down and maybe therefore more action is possible—or at least hope of action. Paul and Joe in the shadow of the wings of the Angel of Death, looking out of their private agony into the world's public agony:

J.C: I want to be surrounded by a warmhearted Jewish family.
E.B.: Our work is to stop the war.
P.G.: The kids aren't beautiful. They aren't sexy. I trust my body.

Meanwhile Joe plans a play on war resistance for high-school kids. And Paul gnaws away at the walls.

The pressures and the packing accelerate as we visit these three people, but we had to talk to the few who were left.

MARCH 31, 1969:

At 800 West End Avenue the pressure mounts with the packing. The rooms are full of visitors, journalists, friends, family.
Julian has the flu and his cousin Wilbur comes with a doctoral manner and prescribes.
Larry Berkowitz comes and tells dramatically about the bust at the *Che* performance, as if Julian's mother were accustomed to all the dirty words.
There are two kinds of friends who alternately repeat warnings: Stay here. Leave fast. Stay here. Leave now.
We pack all night. Certain things, the theatre archives, certain books we feel are going to Europe to stay. There are unanswerable questions about when, if ever, we are coming back.
All well and good to say that you can ask that every time you leave a room, but there is something eerie about leaving America now. There's all this tension/revolutionary fervor/impending violence.
Because Isha had the flu I missed the last performance. Our last performance was *Frankenstein,* and I think of how appropriate it is that it ends with a countdown:
10 9 8 7 6 5 4 3 2 1

America,
Our parting word was: Zero.

APRIL 1, 1969:

SS Europa. Embarking. Tears. Kisses.
The ship is not like the student ship. The passengers are middle-aged Germans on the last lap of a Caribbean cruise.
No news of the outside world: the ship's news tells us nothing.
Isha understands what the ship is, and what the sea is.
Luke and Günter befriend the crew.
Günter writes a manifesto which the crew helps mimeograph and post.
And all the time at sea we try to find a restrospect on the American scene. And some cohesive picture about what's happening in the United States.
But the images are disconnected, even here in the Atlantic's No Man's Land:
The turn towards violence.
The seething of the black revolution.

The turn towards 'ecstasy' as a form of 'depolarization' for the discouraged.

The ambivalence of the man on the street.

The toughening of the cops.

The tightening of the media.

The extreme sensitivity to the political content of everything: clothes, foods, architecture, ads, songs.

The escalation of demands: The real demands are unspoken. The primary demands are not the final demands. The escalation is towards the final demand for autonomy. The schools are an example. The intellectuals are an example.

The blacks are not just an example: The blacks are for real.

The terrible whispering in the grass.

The grass roots burning with fire and static:

> In the city every match is a weapon.
> The paranoia sees CIA men at every lunch counter.
> 'Everyone' fears that he underestimates what the blacks are secretly doing.
> 'Everyone' fears that he exaggerates what the blacks are secretly doing.

The great opposing camp, the Establishment, of which each component man is halfway on the side of peace/love, but committed to fear and greed.
The schoolchildren wanting to make a world that they can really live in, and refusing to settle for less.

> The frightening realization that one strong voice could turn things either way. There is no strong voice.

APRIL 3, 1969:

The third night out we celebrate the Seder, all crowding into our cabin:

> With Matzohs, the Bread of Affliction, and eggs in salt water, and apples and honey and nuts and Bitter Herbs.
> And the retelling of the Passover story of our liberation and exodus from the fleshpots of the House of Bondage.

The high seas. The first breath taken.

INDEX